T0323881

Samuel Fuller: Interviews

Conversations with Filmmakers Series
Gerald Peary, General Editor

Samuel Fuller
INTERVIEWS

Edited by Gerald Peary

University Press of Mississippi / Jackson

www.upress.state.ms.us

The University Press of Mississippi is a member
of the Association of American University Presses.

Copyright © 2012 by University Press of Mississippi
All rights reserved
Manufactured in the United States of America

First printing 2012
∞

Library of Congress Cataloging-in-Publication Data

Fuller, Samuel, 1912–1997.
  Samuel Fuller: interviews / edited by Gerald Peary.
    p. cm. — (Conversations with filmmakers series)
  Includes bibliographical references and index.
  ISBN 978-1-61703-306-3 (cloth : alk. paper) — ISBN 978-1-61703-307-0 (ebook)
  ISBN 978-1-4968-5799-6 (paperback)
  1. Fuller, Samuel, 1912–1997—Interviews. I. Title.
  PN1998.3.F85A3 2012
  791.4302'33092—dc23   2011044957

British Library Cataloging-in-Publication Data available

Contents

Introduction

Pickup on South Street, Verboten!, Shock Corridor, The Naked Kiss. Do these loopy film titles mean anything to you? For a committed Fullerite, those four works with risible names, all produced on miniscule "B" budgets, are undisputed masterpieces, a quartet of American classics. And for the uninitiated public? To state the obvious, the late Sam Fuller, ace film-maker, isn't for everybody, or probably most people. And being cultured and educated might just get in the way.

Fuller, who made twenty-three features between 1949 and 1989, is the very definition of a "cult" director, appreciated by those with a certain bent of subterranean taste, a penchant for what Manny Farber famously labeled as "termite art." The French critic Luc Moullet explained, "In Fuller, we see everything that other directors deliberately excise from their films: disorder, filth, the unexplainable, the stubbly chin, and a kind of fascinating ugliness in a man's face."[1] Lee Server, a Fuller expert and devotee: "His filmography is a unique paradox: work born for the most part in the lower depths of the 'B' movie mills, yet shot with elements seldom seen outside of the avant-garde and 'art' film: autobiography, thematic obsessions, and technical experimentation."[2]

Artsy, yes, but not in an obvious, palatable way.

You've got to appreciate low-budget, pulpish genre films, including westerns and war movies, and make room for some hard-knuckle, ugly bursts of violence. You've also got to make allowance for lots of broad, crass acting, and scripts (all Fuller-written) which can be stiff, sometimes campy, sometimes laboriously didactic. And if your aesthetic requires a "positive" person in the narrative to root for? Opt for a less irregular director. *I Shot Jesse James* (1949), Fuller's first feature, for which he was writer-director, set the stage for an abiding interest in dramatizing the lives of the fatally damned, the certifiably psychopathic. His "hero," Bob Ford, is the "dirty little coward" who plugged Jesse in the back, and then, on stage, reenacted the sleazy murder for fame and money.

Fuller's protagonists are, most often, creepy and off-putting, paranoid individualists with what we call today "anger issues." O'Meara, the disgruntled, post–Civil War outcast in *Run of the Arrow* (1957), speaks for many a bitter Fuller lead: "I hate, Mama, I hate . . . I am a rebel because I want to be." Sam Fuller might be the only American filmmaker who said "No" to casting John Wayne. The worry was that "the Duke" would turn Fuller's fervently anti-war war film, *The Big Red One* (1980), into a patriotic, heroic work. Lee Server: "Fuller's military men are almost always deeply flawed, ambivalent, or outright crazy."[3]

So who speaks for Sam Fuller, and his very strange oeuvre? Film critics around the world. Even more, filmmakers. There has never been a "B" director who has been so embraced, and revered, by "A"-level cineastes. From the 1960s until his death in 1997, he was befriended by an amazing conglomerate of directors. Among them: Jim Jarmusch, Sara Driver, Martin Scorsese, Steven Spielberg, Jonathan Demme, Peter Bogdanovich, Curtis Hanson, Quentin Tarantino, Francis Ford Coppola, John Cassavetes, Wim Wenders, Rainer Werner Fassbinder, François Truffaut, Jean-Luc Godard.

It was a great kick for filmmakers, hanging with the crusty old storyteller. Much more important, his cinema amazed them. Fuller put the punch back into movies, shooting and cutting in wild ways that surprised even the most mannered, self-consciously formalist filmmakers.

Credit Fuller's early employ as a New York crime reporter for giving him a unique slant on making cinema. He saw the motion pictures as a boiling-hot medium in line with the excitement of a tabloid front page: bold headlines, sensational photographs, lurid leads. His filmmaker peers responded to the yellow-journalism audacity of Fuller's imagery: the shot from the grave—POV of a dead man—in *Forty Guns*, the sordid attack of the "nymphos" in *Shock Corridor* (1963), the bizarre bald hooker in *The Naked Kiss* (1964). Grab the audience—that was Fuller's credo. As he put it in his famous cigar-chomping cameo in Godard's *Pierrot le fou* (1965): "Film is like a battleground . . . love, hate, violence, death. In a single word: emotion."

Godard readily acknowledged that he lifted an extreme close-up of a revolver in *Breathless* (1959) from a bold shot in Fuller's western, *Forty Guns* (1957). And Truffaut, soon after making *The 400 Blows* (1959), wrote of Fuller's *Verboten!* (1959), "I realize I still have to learn how to dominate a film perfectly, to give it rhythm and style, to bring out the poetry as simply as possible without forcing it. . . . I shall go to this film again because I always come away from Sam Fuller films both admiring and jealous."[4]

Over forty years later, in an introduction to *A Third Face*, Fuller's 2002 posthumous autobiography, Martin Scorsese discussed *his* indebtedness. "I loved Sam as a filmmaker," Scorsese said, "and it's impossible for me to imagine my own work without his influence and example." (Isn't *Taxi Driver*'s violent, estranged Travis Bickle a refugee from the Fuller universe?) Where others saw flaws, Scorsese saw sinewy strength. "Sure, Sam's movies are blunt, pulpy, occasionally crude, lacking any sense of delicacy or subtlety. But those aren't shortcomings. They're simply reflections of his temperament."

For Scorsese, there's nothing amiss with Fuller. "I think if you don't like the films of Sam Fuller, than you don't like cinema," he asserted. "Or at least you don't understand it."

Scorsese's point has merit. Fuller is a *cinematic* director above all, deftly combining orchestrated long takes and elegant tracking shots with sudden, brash montage jolts: idiosyncratic cuts, feverish close-ups. Phil Hardy, author of the 1970 book *Samuel Fuller*, tried to explain: "Just as violence is at the core of Fuller's world, so his style centers on the violent yoking-together of disparate elements. . . . The essence of Fuller's style lies in creating dramatic confrontations by disrupting the spatial unity of a scene; the sacrifice of external naturalism to internal landscape. . . . Fuller's treatment of his world always makes of it an interior landscape through which his characters trek."

But how did Fuller come to have such a startling filmic vision? He was a high school dropout whose training was in journalism, not movie-making. His most deeply felt experience was being a soldier fighting World War II.

The prism by which many critics have "understood" Fuller is in classifying him as a "primitive," an outsider artist. A Henri Rousseau, perhaps, a genius naïf.

The "primitive" branding started in a 1959 essay by Luc Moullet in *Cahiers du Cinéma*, and, in 1960, Truffaut affirmed it in the same periodical. It traveled to the US via Andrew Sarris in the seminal 1963 *Film Culture* essay on "American Directors," his thoughts repeated verbatim in the ever-quoted 1968 book, *The American Cinema*. "Fuller is an American primitive whose works have to be seen to be understood, not heard or synopsized. . . . It is time the cinema followed the other arts in honoring its primitives."

"The most common word applied to your films is 'primitive.' Do you like that?" the filmmaker was asked in 1980 by scholars Peter Lehman and Russell Merritt. Fuller's reply was good-natured, bemused. "It doesn't bother me at all," he said. "In a way it intrigues me. It gives me a picture of a hairy ape and a grabber of women's hair."

But "primitive" has a better connotation for Fuller fans. It doesn't imply stupid, sexist, brutish. Fuller films have *content*. They are about important considerations. In praising *Verboten!*, a fiction film set at the Nuremberg trial, Truffaut championed Fuller as a "committed filmmaker," and compared him to Balzac.[5] Scorsese, too, was taken by Fuller's thematic ambition. "[Sam] . . . was always trying to fathom the unfathomable, whether it was a subject as broad as the inhumanity of war or the injustice of racism, or, on a more personal level, the thirst for power or the infectiousness of paranoia. . . . I think he was one of the bravest and most profoundly moral artists the movies have ever had."[6]

This was no modest, reticent, retiring filmmaker. Samuel Fuller liked to talk. And talk. All who interviewed him got their money's worth. The conversations were always energized, slangy, racy, uninhibited, as Fuller rattled on and on and on, happily gabbing about the movies he made and, just as enthusiastically, providing the minute plot points of the movies he wished to make. Always, he had colorful, unusual scripts ready to go before the camera. And he had hundreds of "yarns" (his favored word) to spill. Should he tell you about working in Hollywood with Zanuck? Or fighting through the War with his battalion, the Big Red One? Or perhaps about his unfilmed screenplay for Baudelaire's *Flowers of Evil*? Or what a nice gal was Marilyn Monroe, who went on a date with his brother? (All of this while huffing and puffing on his ubiquitous cigar.)

This was great material for the inevitably charmed interviewer, who really didn't have to do much but nod and listen to Fuller's raspy, demonstrative speechifying. The wearisome chore came afterward, when faced with endless tapes demanding to be transcribed—all those Fuller words! I know of at least one case where a film scholar just gave up on doing anything with his bundle of tape recordings. He'd asked Fuller to tell his life from the beginning, and, after many hours of recorded talk, the filmmaker was still caught up in relating his childhood.

Perhaps Fuller was making up for the years when nobody asked him anything. He started directing in Hollywood in an era when directors—Cecil B. DeMille, the exception—were barely noticed by the public; and he hardly made the kind of prestigious movies which might bring in the press. Interestingly, a reporter for the *Motion Picture Herald* did visit Fuller at his Laurel Canyon office in June 1949, shortly after he finished *I Shot Jesse James*. It's a very odd interview, all paraphrasing of the filmmaker. William R. Weaver didn't allow Fuller the courtesy of a single quote, though acknowledging that Fuller offered "fifty-thousand greased light-ning words" about his upcoming projects. Flash ahead to 1958, where Fuller finally got to speak a little, for a story in the *Newark Evening News*. He talked lovingly of the Big Red One, his old infantry regiment. "Alfred Hitchcock puts himself into every picture as his trademark," Fuller said, "I put my infantry division into my pictures."

Who had noticed him at this point? In America, it was only Manny Farber, writing in *The Nation*. In 1952, Farber lauded Fuller's "skepti-cism and energy," and included the Korean War drama, *Fixed Bayonets*, among "The Best Films of 1951." Farber's mini-review: "Funny, morbid. The best war film since *Bataan*. I wouldn't mind seeing it seven times." Internationally, Fuller first became known when *Pickup on South Street* (1953) actually won a Bronze Lion at the Venice Film Festival, over the political objections of jury president, Luchino Visconti. The award was attacked by many Europeans. They felt, though Fuller denied it, that the movie was an anti-Communist tract. Among the most vociferous oppo-nents of the film was the esteemed French Marxist, Georges Sadoul.

And that might be a major reason that the young Gallic critics around *Cahiers du Cinéma*, who were avowedly anti-ideological, embraced Sam Fuller. In a December 1954 article in *Arts*, François Truffaut noted his af-fection for *I Shot Jesse James*, *The Steel Helmet* (1951), and *Fixed Bayonets*. In a Christmas 1955 *Cahiers*, Eric Rohmer included Fuller in a list of "the age of auteurs" in Hollywood. Godard said later, ". . . [We] fought very of-ten for our sort of American cinema—a small one. We preferred Samuel Fuller and Budd Boetticher to William Wyler and George Stevens."[7] In a November 1957 *Cahiers*, Godard reviewed *Forty Guns* and described it with the kind of hyperbole which the *Cahiers* critics slathered on their favorites: "Each scene, each shot of this savage and brutal Western . . . is so rich in invention . . . and so bursting with daring conceptions that it reminds one of the extravagances of Abel Gance and Stroheim, or purely and simply of Murnau."

Fuller's "B" films in a league with the cinema classics of Gance, Stro-heim, Murnau? The *Cahiers* crowd's polemicizing worked. Sam Fuller was lionized as a major "auteur." In the US, Andrew Sarris placed Fuller in the elevated category of "The Far Side of Paris" in *The American Cin-ema*, alongside such director luminaries as Capra, Preminger, Sturges, Minnelli, and, again, Stroheim. In Britain, the young academic-trained writers at *Movie* claimed Fuller as eminently worthy of study and wrote in praise of his films.

And finally the interviews came. They were conducted by critics who had studied up on Fuller's works and were thrilled to meet him and rave about his oeuvre. In 1965 Swedish critic Stig Bjorkman talked to him in Paris, and their detailed conversation was printed later in *Movie*, Winter 1969–70. In 1967 Fuller was interviewed by *Cahiers du Cinéma* for French television. In 1968 two knowledgeable Americans, Eric Sherman and Martin Rubin, met at length with Fuller for inclusion in their book, *The Director's Event*. In 1969 the Edinburgh Film Festival brought Fuller to Scotland as a special guest, and he was the subject of a group interview with eight of England's most important critics. Sam Fuller, celebrity.

Also for Edinburgh, Peter Wollen and David Will were commissioned to edit a book about him, *Samuel Fuller*. Two other British books on Fuller's movies came out shortly after, Phil Hardy's *Samuel Fuller* (1970) and Nicholas Garnham's *Samuel Fuller* (1971). Erudite French studies followed in the 1980s, by Olivier Amiel, François Guerif, and Jean Narboni and Noel Simsolo. In the 1990s, two excellent Fuller studies were published in America, Lee Server's *Samuel Fuller: Film Is a Battleground* (1994) and Lisa Dombrowski's *If You Die, I'll Kill You* (2008). Finally, there's Fuller's marvelous autobiography, *A Third Face* (2002), published five years after Fuller's 1997 death.

Even when his career slowed, the interviews kept coming. Fuller kept talking. In 1980, at the release of *The Big Red One*, Fuller agreed to meet with the press, helping with the film's publicity. This is when I met with him, at his LA smoke-filled home, The Shack. As everyone else, I was taken by his tremendous friendliness and startling openness. But what he didn't acknowledge, the good soldier, was how heartbroken he really was that *The Big Red One*, his most personal, autobiographical work, had been severely cut, deeply wrecked, by the Lorimar producers.

And Samuel Fuller's reputation today? It was certainly enhanced by the unveiling of a restored, reconstructed version of *The Big Red One* at the 2004 Cannes Film Festival, under the guidance of critic Richard Schickel. In my original review of the film, I'd given it a disappointing "two stars." The new version, close to the filmmaker's vision, seemed almost a masterpiece. If only Fuller had survived to be feted at Cannes!

For their help with this book, I would like to thank John Hall, Geoffrey Macnab, Richard Jameson, Richard Schickel, Joseph McBride, Jim Jarmusch, Sara Driver, Kenneth Greenberg, Robert Rosenthal, Quentin Miller, Michele Plott, Lisa Nesselson, Martin Rubin, Eric Sherman, Jackie Sand, Selene Rosenberg, Seetha Srinivasan at the University Press of Mississippi for approving this project, and Leila Salisbury for patiently seeing it through.

With thanks to my fabulous wife, Amy Geller. In memory of Karen Schmeer and Peter Brunette, both of whom are missed incredibly.

GP

Notes

1. Luc Moullet, "Sam Fuller: In Marlowe's Footsteps," *Cahiers du Cinéma*, March 1959.

2. Lee Server, *Sam Fuller: Film Is a Battleground* (Jefferson, N.C.: McFarland & Co., Inc., 1994).

3. Ibid.

4. François Truffaut, *The Films in My Life* (New York: Simon & Schuster, 1978).

5. Ibid.

6. Martin Scorsese, introduction to *A Third Face: My Tale of Writing, Fighting, and Filmmaking* by Samuel Fuller (New York: Alfred A. Knopf, 2002).

7. Gavin Smith, "Jean-Luc Godard," *Film Comment*, March–April 1996.

Chronology

1912   Born August 12, in Worcester, Massachusetts, the son of Benjamin Rabinovitch and Rebecca Baum, Jewish immigrants. The family name had been changed to Fuller.

1923   Family moves to New York, at the death of Fuller's father.

1924   Works as a copy boy at age twelve for the *New York Evening Journal*.

1928   Becomes a crime reporter for the *New York Evening Graphic* at age seventeen.

1931   Quits the *Graphic* and hitchhikes around the US, doing occasional freelance journalism.

1934   Gets a temporary job as a crime reporter for the *San Francisco Chronicle*, then moves to editorial writing for the *San Diego Sun*.

1935   Returns to New York and publishes a pulp novel, *Burn, Baby, Burn*, about the execution of a pregnant woman.

1936   Publishes a second novel, *Test Tube Baby*, about a young man born through artificial insemination. Gets a screenwriting credit for *Hats Off*, a musical about rival press agents which veers far from his script.

1937   Moves to Los Angeles. Writes screenplay for *It Happened in Hollywood*, about a cowboy actor who doesn't want to play a screen gangster and disappoint his child fans. Fuller: "My first real credit on a picture."

1938   Screenplays for *Gangs of New York* and *Adventure in Sahara*. Publishes *Make Up and Kiss*, a fictional exposé of cosmetics companies.

1939   Screenplay for *Federal Man-Hunt*.

1940   Screenplay for *Bowery Boy*.

1941   Screenplay for *Confirm and Deny*. On December 8, the day after Pearl Harbor, Fuller enlists in the US Army.

1942   Assigned to the 26th Regiment, Third Battalion, Company K, known as the Big Red One. He is shipped to Algeria in November, where his battalion proceeds to fight the Germans across North Africa.

1943   In February, his battalion is routed by Rommel in the Kesserine Pass, Tunisia. The Big Red One fights back and, in May, helps take the city of Tunis and defeat the Nazis and Fascists in Africa. In July, the Big Red One lands in Sicily. After many battles, they are reassigned to Liverpool, for seven months of strategic drills. In Hollywood, Fuller's pre-War screenplay is used for *Power of the Press*.

1944   Participates in the D-Day invasion on Omaha Beach, Normandy. Fuller: "Of the 183 men who'd landed with my company, about a hundred were dead, wounded, or missing in action." He fights the retreating Germans across France and Belgium. Publication in the USA of his long-completed mystery novel, *The Dark Page*.

1945   Participates in the US Army action taking towns across Germany. At the liberation of the German concentration camp in Czecho-slavakia at Falkenau, he shoots 16mm footage. In September, Fuller docks in Boston and, soon after, returns to Hollywood. *Gangs of the Waterfront* is produced, using a prewar Fuller script.

1946   Marries Martha Downes.

1949   *I Shot Jesse James*, his first credit as a director. Screenplay for *Shockproof*.

1950   Directs *The Baron of Arizona*.

1951   Directs his first acclaimed movie, *The Steel Helmet*, set in the Korean War. Also directs *Fixed Bayonets*. Screenplay for *Tanks Are Coming*.

1952   Directs *Park Row*, a semi-autobiographical salute to the newspaper business. Screenplay for *Scandal Sheet*, based on his novel, *The Dark Page*.

1953   Directs *Pickup on South Street*, which wins a Bronze Lion at the Venice Film Festival. Screenplay for *The Command*.

1954   Directs *Hell and High Water*, his first film shot in Cinemascope.

1955   Directs *House of Bamboo*, filmed on location in Japan.

1957   Directs *Run of the Arrow*, *China Gate*, and *Forty Guns*.

1959   Directs *Verboten!* and *The Crimson Kimono*. Divorces Martha Downes Fuller.

1961   Directs *Underworld U.S.A.*

1962   Directs *Merrill's Marauders*.

1963   Directs *Shock Corridor*.

1964   Directs *The Naked Kiss*.

1965   Appears as himself in Jean-Luc Godard's *Pierrot le fou*. He is honored with an evening at the Cinémathèque Française.

1967   Marries German actress, Christa Lang. Co-writes *The Cape Town Affair*, which is *Pickup on South Street* moved to South Africa.

1969   Directs *Shark!*, but, due to production compromises, wants his name taken off this picture.

1971   Appears in Dennis Hopper's *The Last Movie*.

1972   Directs in Germany *Dead Pigeon on Beethoven Street*, starring his wife, Christa Lang.

1974   Co-writes *The Klansmen*.

1975   A daughter, Samantha, is born.

1977   Appears in Wim Wenders's *An American Friend*.

1979   Appears in Steven Spielberg's *1941*.

1980   Directs *The Big Red One*, which was released in a cut-down version.

1982   Directs *White Dog*, which, because of controversy over its racial politics, is kept from release by Paramount Pictures. Angered, Fuller moves with his wife and daughter to Paris, France. He appears in Wim Wenders's *The State of Things*.

1984   Directs in France *Les Voleurs de la Nuit/Thieves After Dark*, selected for the Berlin Film Festival. Appears in Steven Paul's *Slapstick (Of Another Kind)*. He publishes in Europe an adventure novel, *La Grand Melee*.

1987   Appears in Mika Kaurismaki's *Helsinki Napoli—All Night Long*.

1988   Appears in Larry Cohen's *Salem's Lot*.

1989   Directs for a French production company *Street of No Return*, shot in Lisbon.

1990   Directs in France two television movies, *Le Jour du châtiment/The Day of Reckoning* and *The Madonna and the Dragon*.

1995   He, Christa, and Samatha return to the USA, and to The Shack, their ex-LA home. Felled by a stroke, he works on an autobiography.

1997   Appears in Wim Wenders's *The End of Violence*, a final screen role. Fuller dies on October 30. In November, a Directors Guild memorial tribute.

2002   Posthumous publication of his autobiography, *A Third Face*, by Alfred A. Knopf. The book was finished by Christa Lang Fuller and Jerome Henry Rudes.

2004   A restored, full-length version of *The Big Red One* is shown at the Cannes Film Festival.

Filmography

1948
I SHOT JESSE JAMES
Lippert Productions
Director: **Samuel Fuller**
Screenplay: **Samuel Fuller**
Executive Producer: Robert Lippert
Producer: Carl Hittleman
Cinematography: Ernest Miller
Editing: Paul Landres
Music: Albert Glasser (Song by Katherine Glasser)
Art Direction: Frank Hotaling
Assistant Director: Johnny Grubbs
Set Decoration: James Redd, John McCarthy
Cast: John Ireland (Bob Ford), Preston Foster (John Kelley), Barbara Britton (Cynthy Waters), Reed Hadley (Jesse James), J. Edward Bromberg (Harry Kane), Tom Tyler (Frank James), Victor Kilian (Soapy), Barbara Woodell (Mrs. Zee James), Tom Noonan (Charles Ford), Byron Foulger (Room Clerk), Eddie Dunn (Bartender), Jeni Le Gon (Maid), Phil Pine (Man in Saloon), Robin Short (Troubadour), Margia Dean (Singer in Bar), Gene Collins (Young Man)
35mm, B&W, 81 minutes

1949
THE BARON OF ARIZONA
Lippert Productions
Director: **Samuel Fuller**
Screenplay: **Samuel Fuller**
Producer: Carl Hittleman
Cinematography: James Wong Howe
Editing: Arthur Hilton
Music: Paul Dunlap

Art Direction: P. Frank Sylos
Assistant Director: Frank Fox
Set Decoration: Otto Siegel, Ray Robinson
Costumes: Alfred Berke, Kitty Mayor
Cast: Vincent Price (James Addison Reavis), Ellen Drew (Sofia Peralta-Reavis), Beulah Bondi (Lorna Morales), Reed Hadley (John Griff), Vladimir Sokoloff (Pepito Alvarez), Robert Barratt (Judge Adams), Robin Short (Lansing), Barbara Woodell (Carry Lansing), Tina Rome (Rita), Margia Dean (Marquesa), Edward Keane (Surveyor Miller), Gene Roth (Father Guardian), Karen Kester (Sofia as child), Joseph Green, Fred Kohler, Jr., Tristram Coffin, I. Stanford Jolley, Terry Frost, Angelo Rosito, Zachery Yaconelli, Adolfo Ornelas, Wheaton Chambers, Robert O'Neill, Stephen Harrison, Stuart Holmes, Jonathan Hale
35mm, B&W, 90 minutes

1950
THE STEEL HELMET
Lippert Productions
Director: **Samuel Fuller**
Screenplay: **Samuel Fuller**
Executive Producer: Robert Lippert
Producer: **Samuel Fuller**
Associate Producer: William Berke
Cinematography: Ernest Miller
Editing: Philip Cahn
Music: Paul Dunlap
Art Direction: Theobald Holsopple
Assistant Director: John Francis Murphy
Set Decoration: Clarence Steenson
Costumes: Alfred Berke
Cast: Gene Evans (Sergeant Zack), Robert Hutton (Private Bronte), Richard Loo ((Sergeant Tanaka), Steve Brodie (Lieutenant Driscoll), James Edwards (Corporal Thompson), William Chun ("Short Round"), Richard Monahan (Private Baldy), Harold Fong (The Red), Sid Melton, Neyle Morrow, Lynn Stallmaster
35mm, B&W, 84 minutes

1951
FIXED BAYONETS
Twentieth Century-Fox

Director: **Samuel Fuller**
Screenplay: **Samuel Fuller**
Producer: Jules Buck
Cinematography: Lucien Ballard
Editing: Nick De Maggio
Music: Roy Webb
Musical Director: Lionel Newman
Orchestration: Maurice de Packh
Art Directors: Lyle Wheeler, George Patrick
Sound: Eugene Grossman, Harry M. Leonard
Assistant Director: Paul Melnick
Set Decoration: Thomas Little, Fred J. Rhode
Costumes: Charles Le Maire
Cast: Richard Basehart (Corporal Denno), Gene Evans (Sergeant Rock), Michael O'Shea (Sergeant Lonergan), Richard Hylton (Private Wheeler), Craig Hill (Lieutenant Gibbs), Skip Homeier (Whitey), Henry Kulky (Vogl), Richard Monahan (Walowicz), Paul Richards (Ramirez), George Wesley (Griff), Tony Kent (Mainotes), Don Orlando (Borcellino), Patrick Fitzgibbon (Paddy), Neyle Morrow (Medic), Mel Pogue (Bulchek), George Conrad (Zablocki), David Wolfson, Buddy Thorpe, Al Negbo, Wyott Ordung, Bill Hickman, James Dean
35mm, B&W, 92 minutes

1952
PARK ROW
Samuel Fuller Productions/United Artists
Director: **Samuel Fuller**
Screenplay: **Samuel Fuller**
Producer: **Samuel Fuller**
Cinematography: Jack Russell
Editing: Philip Cahn
Music: Paul Dunlap
Art Direction: Theobald Holsopple
Sound: Earl Crain, Sr.
Assistant Director: Joseph Depew
Set Decoration: Ray Robinson
Costumes: Jack Miller
Cast: Gene Evans (Phineas Mitchell), Mary Welch (Charity Hackett), Bela Kovacs (Ottmar Mergenthaler), Herbert Heyes (Josiah Davenport), Tina Rome (Jenny O'Rourke), George O'Hanlon (Steve Brodie), J. M.

Kerrigan (Dan O'Rourke), Forrest Taylor (Charles Leach), Don Orlando (Mr. Angelo), Neyle Morrow (Thomas Guest), Dick Elliott, Stuart Randall, Dee Pollock, Hal K. Dawson, Charles Horvath
35mm, B&W, 83 minutes

1953
PICKUP ON SOUTH STREET
Twentieth Century-Fox
Director: **Samuel Fuller**
Screenplay: **Samuel Fuller**, from a story by Dwight Taylor
Producer: Jules Schermer
Cinematography: Joe MacDonald
Editing: Nick De Maggio
Music: Leigh Harline
Musical Director: Lionel Newman
Orchestration: Edward Powell
Art Direction: Lyle Wheeler, George Patrick
Sound: Winston H. Leverett, Harry M. Leonard
Assistant Director: Ad Schaumer
Set Decoration: Al Orenbach
Costumes: Charles Le Maire, Travilla
Cast: Richard Widmark (Skip McCoy), Jean Peters (Candy), Thelma Ritter (Moe Williams), Murvyn Vye (Captain Tiger), Richard Kiley (Joey), Willis Bouchey (Zara), Milburn Stone (Wineki), Henry Slate (MacGregor), Victor Perry (Lightnin' Louie), Jerry O'Sullivan (Enyart), Harry Carter (Dietrich), George E. Stone (Clerk), George Eldredge (Fenton), Stuart Randall (Police Commissioner), Frank Kumagi (Lum), George Berkeley, Emmett Lynn, Maurice Samuels, Parley Baer, Jav Loftlin, Virginia Carroll, Roger Moore
35mm, B&W, 80 minutes

1954
HELL AND HIGH WATER
Twentieth Century-Fox
Director: **Samuel Fuller**
Screenplay: Jesse L. Lasky, Jr., **Samuel Fuller,** from a story by David Hempstead
Producer: Raymond A. Klune
Cinematography: Joe MacDonald

Editing: James B. Clark
Music: Alfred Newman (song lyrics by Harry Powell)
Orchestration: Edward B. Powell
Art Direction: Lyle Wheeler, Leland Fuller
Sound: Eugene Grossman, Roger Heman
Assistant Director: Ad Schaumer
Set Decoration: Walter M. Scott, Stuart Reiss
Costumes: Charles Le Maire, Travilla
Cast: Richard Widmark (Adam Jones), Bella Darvi (Denise Montel), Cameron Mitchell (Brodski), Victor Francen (Professor Montel), Gene Evans (Holter), David Wayne (Walker), Richard Loo (Fujimori), Stephen Bekassy (Neuman), Wong Artarne (Chin Lee), Rollin Moriyama (Joto), William Yip (Ho Sin)
35mm, Color, Cinemascope, 103 minutes

1955
HOUSE OF BAMBOO
Twentieth Century-Fox
Director: **Samuel Fuller**
Screenplay: Harry Kleiner, **Samuel Fuller**
Producer: Buddy Adler
Cinematography: Joe MacDonald
Editing: James B. Clark
Music: Leigh Harline (song by Leigh Harline, Jack Brooks)
Musical Director: Lionel Newman
Orchestration: Edward B. Powell
Art Direction: Lyle Wheeler, Addison Hehr
Sound: John D. Stack, Harry M. Leonard
Assistant Director: David Silver
Set Decoration: Walter M. Scott, Stuart Reiss
Costumes: Charles Le Maire
Cast: Robert Stack (Eddie Spanier/Kenner), Robert Ryan (Sandy Dawson), Shirley Yamaguchi (Mariko), Cameron Mitchell (Griff), Brad Dexter (Captain Hanson), Sessue Hayakawa (Inspector Kito), Biff Elliott (Webber), Sandro Giglio (Ceran), Elko Hanabusa (Japanese screaming woman), DeForest Kelley (Charlie), Peter Gray (Willy), Robert Quarry (Phil), John Doucette, Teru Shimada, Robert Hosoi, Jack Maeshiro, May Takasugi, Neyle Morrow, Reiko Hayakawa, Sandy Ozeka
35mm, Color, Cinemascope, 102 minutes

1957
RUN OF THE ARROW
Globe Enterprises/RKO
Director: **Samuel Fuller**
Screenplay: **Samuel Fuller**
Producer: **Samuel Fuller**
Cinematography: Joseph Biroc
Editing: Gene Fowler, Jr.
Music: Victor Young
Art Direction: Albert D'Agostino, Jack Okey
Sound: Virgil Smith
Assistant Director: Ben Chapman
Set Decoration: Bert Granger
Cast: Rod Steiger (O'Meara), Sarita Montiel (Yellow Moccasin), Brian
Keith (Captain Clark), Ralph Meeker (Lieutenant Driscoll), Jay C. Flip-
pen (Walking Coyote), Charles Bronson (Blue Buffalo), Olive Carey
(Mrs. O'Meara), Col. Tim McCoy (General Allen), H. M. Wynant (Crazy
Wolf), Neyle Morrow (Lieutenant Stockwell), Frank Dekova (Red
Cloud), Stuart Randall (Colonel Taylor), Frank Warner, Billy Miller,
Chuck Hayward, Carleton Young, Chuck Roberson, Angie Dickinson
(Yellow Moccasin, voice)
35mm, Technicolor, 86 minutes

1957
CHINA GATE
Globe Enterprises/Twentieth Century-Fox
Director: **Samuel Fuller**
Screenplay: **Samuel Fuller**
Producer: **Samuel Fuller**
Cinematography: Joseph Biroc
Editing: Gene Fowler, Jr., Dean Harrison
Music: Victor Young and Max Steiner (song by Victor Young, Harold
Adamson)
Art Direction: John Mansbridge
Sound Editing: Bert Schoenfeld
Assistant Director: Harold E. Knox
Costumes: Henry West, Beau Van den Ecker
Cast: Gene Barry (Brock), Angie Dickinson ("Lucky Legs"), Nat "King"
Cole (Goldie), Paul Dubov (Captain Caumont), Lee Van Cleef (Major
Cham), George Givot (Corporal Pigalle), Gerald Milton (Private An-

dreades), Neyle Morrow (Leung), Marcel Dalio (Father Paul), Maurice Marsac (Colonel De Sars), Warren Hsieh (Boy), Paul Busch (Corporal Kruger), Sasha Harden (Private Jazzi), James Hong (Charlie), William Soo Hoo, Weaver Levy, Ziva Rodann
35mm, B&W, Cinemascope, 86 minutes

1957
FORTY GUNS
Globe Enterprises/Twentieth Century-Fox
Director: **Samuel Fuller**
Screenplay: **Samuel Fuller**
Producer: **Samuel Fuller**
Cinematography: Joseph Biroc
Editing: Gene Fowler, Jr.
Music: Harry Sukman (songs by Harry Sukman, Harold Adamson, Victor Young)
Art Direction: John Mansbridge
Sound: Jean Speak, Harry M. Leonard
Assistant Director: Harold E. Knox
Set Decoration: Walter M. Scott, Chester Bayhi
Costumes: Charles Le Maire, Leah Rhodes
Cast: Barbara Stanwyck (Jessica Drummond), Barry Sullivan (Griff Bonnell), Dean Jagger (Ned Logan), John Ericson (Brock Drummond), Gene Barry (Wes Bonnell), Robert Dix (Chico Bonnell), "Jidge" Carroll (Barney Cashman), Paul Dubov (Judge Macy), Gerald Milton (Shotgun Spanger), Ziva Rodann (Rio), Hank Worden (John Chisum), Sandra Wirth (Chico's girlfriend), Neyle Morrow (Wiley), Eve Brent (Louvenia Spanger), Chuck Roberson (Swain), Chuck Hayward (Charlie Savage)
35mm, B&W, Cinemascope, 80 minutes

1959
VERBOTEN!
Globe Enterprises/RKO
Director: **Samuel Fuller**
Screenplay: **Samuel Fuller**
Producer: **Samuel Fuller**
Cinematography: Joseph Biroc
Editing: Philip Cahn
Music: Harry Sukman
Art Direction: John Mansbridge

Sound: Bert Schoenfeld, Jean Speak
Assistant Director: Gordon McLean
Set Decoration: Glen L. Daniels
Costumes: Bernice Pontrelli, Harry West
Cast: James Best (Sgt. David Brent), Susan Cummings (Helga Schiller),
Tom Pittman (Bruno Eckart), Paul Dubov (Captain Harvey), Harold
Daye (Franz), Dick Kallman (Helmuth), Stuart Randall (Colonel), Steven Geray (Burgermeister), Anna Hope (Frau Schiller), Robert Boon (SS Officer), Neyle Morrow (Sergeant Kellogg), Sasha Harden (Erich), Paul
Busch (Guenther), Joseph Turkel, Charles Horvath
35mm, B&W, 93 minutes

1959
THE CRIMSON KIMONO
Globe Enterprises/Columbia
Director: **Samuel Fuller**
Screenplay: **Samuel Fuller**
Producer: **Samuel Fuller**
Cinematography: Sam Leavitt
Editing: Jerome Thoms
Music: Harry Sukman
Orchestration: Jack Hayves, Leo Shuken
Art Direction: William E. Flannery, Robert Boyle
Sound: Josh Westmoreland
Assistant Director: Floyd Joyer
Set Decoration: James Crowe
Costumes: Bernice Pontrelli
Cast: Glenn Corbett (Det. Charlie Bancroft), James Shigeta (Det. Joe Kojaku), Victoria Shaw (Christine Downes), Anna Lee (Mac), Paul Dubov
(Casale), Jaclynne Greene (Roma Wilson), Neyle Morrow (Hansel),
Gloria Pall (Sugar Torch), Barbara Hayden (Mother), George Yoshinaga
(Willy Hidaka), Kaye Elhardt (Nun), Aya Oyama, George Okamura,
Ryosho S. Sogabe, Robert Okazaki, Fuji, Walter Burke
35mm, B&W, 82 minutes

1960
UNDERWORLD U.S.A
Globe Enterprises/Columbia
Director: **Samuel Fuller**
Screenplay: **Samuel Fuller**, from articles by Joseph F. Dineen

Producer: **Samuel Fuller**
Cinematography: Hal Mohr
Editing: Jerome Thoms
Music: Harry Sukman
Art Direction: Robert Peterson
Sound: Charles J. Rice
Assistant Director: Floyd Joyer
Set Decoration: Bill Calvert
Costumes: Bernice Pontrelli
Cast: Cliff Robertson (Tolly Devlin), Beatrice Kay (Sandy), Larry Gates (Driscoll), Richard Rust (Gus), Dolores Dorn (Cuddles), Robert Emhardt (Connors), Paul Dubov (Gela), Gerald Milton (Gunther), Allan Gruener (Smith), David Kent (Young Tolly), Neyle Morrow (Barney), Henry Norell, Sally Mills, Tina Rome, Robert Lieb, Peter Brocco
35mm, B&W, 99 minutes

1962
MERRILL'S MARAUDERS
United States Productions/Warner Bros.
Director: **Samuel Fuller**
Screenplay: **Samuel Fuller**, Milton Sperling, from the book *The Marauders* by Charlton Ogburn, Jr.
Producer: Milton Sperling
Cinematography: William Clothier
Editing: Folmar Blangsted
Music: Howard Jackson
Art Direction: William Magginetti
Sound: Francis M. Stahl
Assistant Director: William Kissel
Cast: Jeff Chandler (Brig. General Frank Merrill), Ty Hardin (Lt. Lee Stockton), Peter Brown (Bullseye), Andrew Duggan (Doc Kolodny), Will Hutchins (Chowhound), Claude Akins (Sgt. Kolowicz), Charles Briggs (Muley), Chuck Roberson, Chuck Hayward, Jack C. Williams, Chuck Hicks, Vaughan Wilson, Pancho Magalona
35mm, Technicolor, Cinemascope, 98 minutes

1963
SHOCK CORRIDOR
Fromkess-Firks/Allied Artists
Director: **Samuel Fuller**

Screenplay: **Samuel Fuller**
Producer: **Samuel Fuller**
Cinematography: Stanley Cortez (hallucinations shot by **Samuel Fuller**)
Editing: Jerome Thoms
Music: Paul Dunlap
Art Direction: Eugene Lourie
Sound: Phil Mitchell
Assistant Director: Floyd Joyer
Set Decoration: Charles Thompson
Costumes: Einar H. Bourman
Cast: Peter Breck (Johnny Barrett), Constance Towers (Cathy), Gene Evans (Boden), James Best (Stuart), Hari Rhodes (Trent), Larry Tucker (Pagliacci), Philip Ahn (Dr. Fong), William Zuckert (Swanee), John Mathews (Dr. Cristo), Neyle Morrow (Psycho), Rachel Romen, Marie Devereux (Nymphos), John Craig, Frankie Gerstle, Paul Dubov, Lucille Curtis, Karen Conrad, Barbara Perry, Marlene Manners, Jeanette Dana, Allison Daniell, Chuck Hicks, Ray Baxter, Linda Barrett, Harry Fleer
35mm, B&W, 101 minutes

1964
THE NAKED KISS
Fromkess-Firks/Allied Artists
Director: **Samuel Fuller**
Screenplay: **Samuel Fuller**
Producer: **Samuel Fuller**
Executive Producers: Leo Fromkess, Sam Firks
Cinematography: Stanley Cortez
Editing: Jerome Thoms
Music: Paul Dunlap
Art Direction: Eugene Lourie
Sound: Alfred J. Overton
Assistant Director: Nate Levinson
Set Decoration: Victor Gangelin
Costumes: Einar H. Bourman, Act III
Cast: Constance Towers (Kelly), Anthony Eisley (Griff), Michael Dante (Grant), Virginia Grey (Candy), Patsy Kelly (Mac), Betty Bronson (Miss Josephine), Marie Devereux (Buff), Karen Conrad (Dusty), Linda Francis (Rembrandt), Barbara Perry (Edna), Betty Robinson (Bunny), Christopher Barry (Peanuts), Walter Mathews (Mike), George Spell (Tim),

Gerald Michenaud (Kip), Patty Robinson (Angel Face), Neyle Morrow (Officer Sam), Monte Mansfield (Farlunde), Fletcher Fist (Barney), Gerald Milton (Zookie), Edy Williams (Hatrack), Sally Mills (Marshmallow), Breena Howaid, Michael Barrere, Patricia Gayle, Sheila Mintz, Bill Sampson
35mm, B&W, 93 minutes

1969
SHARK!*
Heritage Enterprises
Director: **Samuel Fuller**
Screenplay: **Samuel Fuller** and John Kingsbridge, from the novel *His Bones Are Coral* by Victor Canning
Producers: José Luis Calderón, Skip Steloff, Mark Cooper
Post-Production Supervisor: Herbert L. Strock
Cinematography: Raul Martinez Solares
Editing: Carlos Savage
Music: Rafael Moroyoqui
Art Direction: Manuel Fontanals
Cast: Burt Reynolds (Caine), Arthur Kennedy ("Doc"), Barry Sullivan (Professor Dan Mallare), Silvia Pinal (Anna), Carlos Barry ("Runt"), Enrique Lucero (Police Inspector Barok), Manuel Alvarado (Latalia), Francisco Reiguera (Yusef), Emilia Stuart (Asha)
35mm, Eastmancolor, 92 minutes
*Fuller disowned the film, which was taken out of his hands for the editing.

1972
DEAD PIGEON ON BEETHOVEN STREET
Bavaria Atelier Filmgesellschaft
Director: **Samuel Fuller**
Screenplay: **Samuel Fuller**
Cinematography: Jerzy Lipman
Editing: Liesgret Schmitt-Klink
Art Direction: Lothar Kirchem
Cast: Glenn Corbett (Sandy), Christa Lang (Christa), Anton Diffring (Mensur), Eric P. Caspar (Charlie Umlaut), Sieghardt Rupp (Kessin), Alex D'Arcy (Novka), Anthony Ching (Fong), Stéphane Audran
35mm, Color, 102 minutes

1980
THE BIG RED ONE
Lorimar
Director: **Samuel Fuller**
Screenplay: **Samuel Fuller**
Producer: Gene Corman
Cinematography: Adam Greenberg
Editing: David Bretherton, Morton Tubor
Music: Dana Kaproff
Music Supervision: Bodie Chandler
Art Direction: Peter Jamison
Assistant Director: Arne L. Schmidt
2nd Unit Director: Lewis Teague
Cast: Lee Marvin (The Sergeant), Mark Hamill (Griff), Robert Carradine
(Zab), Bobby Di Cicco (Vinci), Kelly Ward (Johnson), Stéphane Audran
(Walloon), Siegfried Rauch (Schroeder), Serge Marquand (Rensonnet),
Charles Macauley (General/Captain), Alain Doutey (Brohan), Maurice
Marsac (Vichy Colonel), Colin Gilbert (Dog Face POW), Joseph Clark,
Ken Campbell, Doug Werner, Perry Lang, Howard Belman, Marthe
Villalonga, Giovanna Galetti, Gregori Biumistre, Shimon Barre, Mattes
Zoffoli, Avraham Ronai, Galit Rotman
35mm, B&W, Metrocolor, 113 minutes

1982
WHITE DOG
Paramount
Director: **Samuel Fuller**
Screenplay: **Samuel Fuller**, Curtis Hanson, from the novella by Ro-
main Gary
Producer: Jon Davison
Cinematography: Bruce Surtees
Editing: Bernard Gribble
Music: Ennio Morricone
Production Design: Brian Eatwell
Assistant Director: William Scott
Set Decoration: Barbara Krieger
Stunt Coordinator: Bob Minor
Cast: Kristy McNichol (Julie Sawyer), Paul Winfield (Keys), Burl Ives
(Carruthers), Jameson Parker (Roland Gray), Marshall Thompson

(Director), Martine Dawson (Martine), Paul Bartel (Cameraman), Neyle Morrow (Soundman), Parley Baer (Wilbur Hull), **Samuel Fuller** (Charlie Felton), Karl Lewis Miller (Attacker), Christa Lang (Nurse), Vernon Weddle (Vet), Helen J. Siff (Pound Operator), Glen Garner (Pound Worker), Tony Brubaker (Sweeper Driver), Hubert Wells (Trainer), Sam Laws (Charlie), Cliff Fellow (Sheriff), Dick Miller, Robert Ritchie (Animal Trainers), Bob Minor (Joe), Samantha Fuller (Helen), Jamie Crowe (Theona)
35mm, Metrocolor, 90 minutes

1982
LES VOLEURS DE LA NUIT/THIEVES AFTER DARK
Parafrance Films
Director: **Samuel Fuller**
Screenplay: **Samuel Fuller** and Olivier Beer, from the novel *Le Chant des Enfants Morts* by Olivier Beer
Producer: Michel Gue
Cinematography: Philippe Rousselot
Editing: Catherine Kelber
Music: Ennio Morricone
Art Direction: Dominique André
Costumes: Sophie Latil
Cast: Véronique Jannot (Isabelle), Bobby Di Cicco (Francois), Victor Lanoux (Inspector), Stéphane Audran (Isabelle's Mother), Claude Chabrol (Louis Crepin), Camille de Casabianca (Corinne Desterne), Andreas Voutsinas (José), Micheline Presle (Morell), **Samuel Fuller** (Zoltan)
35mm, Color, 92 minutes

1989
SAMUEL FULLER'S STREET OF NO RETURN
Thunder Films Intl./FR 3 Films Prod./Animatografo/Instituto Português de Cinema
Director: **Samuel Fuller**
Screenplay: **Samuel Fuller**, Jacques Bral, from the novel by David Goodis
Producer: Jacques Bral
Executive Producers: Jacques-Eric Strauss, Patrick Delauneax, António da Cunha Telles
Editing: Jaques Bral, Jean Dubreuil, Anna Ruiz

Cinematography: Pierre-William Glenn
Music: Karl-Heinz Schafer (song lyrics by **Samuel Fuller**, music by Keith Carradine)
Art Direction: Geoffrey Larcher
Costumes: Olga Pelletier
Cast: Keith Carradine (Michael), Valentina Vargas (Celia), Bill Duke (Borel), Andréa Ferréol (Rhoda), Bernard Fresson (Morin), Marc de Jonge (Eddie), Rebecca Potok (Bertha), Jacques Martial (Gerard), Sérgio Godinho (Pernoy), António Rosário (Meathead), Dominique Hulin (Dablin), Gordon Heath (Black Tramp), Joe Abdo (White Tramp), Trevor Stephens (Lambert), Filipe Ferrer (Gauvreau), Jeremy Boultbee (Doctor), Guilherme Filipe (Policeman), Pedro Nunes (Policeman), Christa Lang (Nurse), Samantha Fuller (Young Fan), Joaquim Miranda (Police Officer), Luís Norton De Matos (Police Officer), **Samuel Fuller** (Chief of Police)
35mm, Fujicolor, 90 minutes

Samuel Fuller: Interviews

Fuller Makes Sleeper
but Can't Tell How

William R. Weaver/1949

From the *Motion Picture Herald*, June 4, 1949.

One gloomy afternoon last January, a dozen trade press reviewers who'd rather have been wasting their time at Santa Anita filed forlornly into a studio projection room. They would watch a little picture garishly entitled *I Shot Jesse James* fall apart in the middle, as such items generally do. But this one didn't. On the contrary, it held this band of reluctant witnesses firmly in its grip for eighty-one attentive minutes, and sent them out asking each other how this could be. Then it went out and did the same thing to the plain people who buy the paid admissions, running up a box-office record likely to establish it as the sleeper of the year.

Now, in a year like this a thing like that prompts investigation; and investigation of *I Shot Jesse James* leads up Laurel Canyon to a house where Samuel Fuller can be interrupted in the headlong preparation of three more pictures scheduled to follow his Screen Guild Productions hit.

Takes Wide-Awake Guy to Develop Sleeper

It turns out that it takes to make a sleeper a very wide-awake guy, not to mention industrious, energetic, and versatile, and that adds up to a quick description of the man surrounded by several thousand source books in a room dominated by a blackboard on the far wall and a triple bank of watercolor sketches flanking same on the right.

You ask him flatly what it was he put into *Jesse* that made it what it became. He replies in about fifty thousand lightning-swift words which inform you completely and with photogenic gestures about *The Baron of Arizona*, now taking shape on the blackboard and in the watercolor

3

sketches, and about *Park Row* and *20,000 Leagues Under the Sea*, which are to follow, but leave your question right where it was when you brought it in. You hold out for something more negotiable, some trick or device or method or policy that can be passed on to others for them to use in making other sleepers.

Story on Screen Precisely What He First Wrote

You persist in your inquiry, and out of the next fifty thousand greased-lightning words come a personal puzzlement as to why anybody who can talk so well, so entertainingly, and so much, prefers to write.

It develops that he's written many pictures, for big studios and top directors, that *Jesse* is the first picture that this writer ever directed, and he holds directorial talent in such high esteem that he undertook his first chore in that field with something like bated breath. One explanation of the success he achieved is the fact that the story the screen told was precisely and without change for better or worse the story born of this man's brain on his typewriter, his blackboard, and in his watercolor sketches. (These last, of a quality warranting a place on anybody's study wall, visualize scenes, sets, characters, and action in detail.)

It by no means follows that the way to make sleepers is to let writers direct all the pictures, for industry history is strewn with tragic disproof of that generality. It appears to have worked out that way in this case. The fact that the Fuller career dates from a stint of employment at twelve years of age as copy boy for Arthur Brisbane could pertain importantly to the man's facility for communication of ideas; but Brisbane had a lot of copy boys who didn't make *Jesse*.

Fuller Emblem: *Big Red One* Signifies Sammy's Wartime Days

James Bacon/1958

From the *Newark Evening News*, June 26, 1958.

Producer-director Sammy Fuller will be the first enlisted man ever to be the main speaker at the annual reunion of the 1st Infantry Division, come August 22 in Rochester, New York. The honor is usually reserved for generals, but Fuller's devotion to The Big Red One has been so uncommon that he was bound to be acknowledged by his wartime buddies.

Like every producer's office in Hollywood, Fuller's is plastered with photographs. There is a difference, however. Instead of movie stars and other celebrities, Fuller's photos are all of officers and men of the 1st Division. There are also citations for the Bronze Star he won in the Sicily landings and the Silver Star he won for Normandy.

Those who know Fuller best say the one-time Hearst reporter prefers to talk about his Division more than his pictures. This is unusual in Hollywood.

"I don't want to sound immodest," he said, "but World War II was won by the 1st Division—and ten replacements."

Since the War, Fuller has made some twenty movies, most of which have plugged his division or regiment. It was easy to do in a war picture like *The Steel Helmet*, but it posed a problem in such as *The Crimson Kimono*, a cops and robbers tale laid in Los Angeles's Little Tokyo, or *Hell and High Water*, a story of the Navy's submarines.

And even more so in *Forty Guns* or *Run of the Arrow*, stories set in the Old West. "The Big Red One," as a division, is only forty-two years old. But the 16th Infantry Regiment, one of the components, goes back to Revolutionary days.

In *The Crimson Kimono*, Fuller shot a scene on a downtown street in front of what was once an Army recruiting poster.

"I substituted the emblem of 'The Big Red One' and let the camera linger on it," he explains.

"But that submarine picture really gave me problems—nothing but sailors in it. Submarine sailors work stripped to the waist, so I tattooed the emblem on one of the guy's arms—in color, too."

In the Westerns, he plugged the 16th Regiment by having soldiers identify themselves as members.

"Alfred Hitchcock puts himself into every picture as his trademark," says Fuller. "I put my infantry division into my pictures."

Samuel Fuller: Interview

Stig Bjorkman/1965

From *Movie* 17 (Winter 1969–70): 25–29. Interview conducted in Paris in 1965. Reprinted by permission of Stig Bjorkman.

Stig Bjorkman: How do you prepare your pictures?

Samuel Fuller: If you notice this blackboard here, you can see that it's separated into columns for the three acts of the film. The fourth column is for the cast. I haven't filled the board yet. Most of it will be written in white chalk. When I introduce a character, I use yellow chalk. When I have a romantic scene, it's blue chalk, and when I have action, violence, it's red chalk. When the whole board is finished, I can sit back and look at it with my crew, and when we see a character that has been introduced a little too late, we can tell easily on the board. Or if we have too many romantic scenes together—two, three lines that are in blue—that's wrong. And if I can end the first act with one or two red lines, the second act with two or three red lines and the third act with four or five red lines, I am going uphill. So I can get a pretty good idea of the balance of the violence and of the romance, or anything I want on the board. That's how I work that.

I first make a very rough sketch of the characters. I don't try to make them look like what I think they should look like. I just get the names up there. Later on, when I have about twenty, thirty pages of the script done, I make portraits. I am an amateur. But I draw the characters the way I visualize them, and I put them up on the wall. I try to cast as close as possible to the portraits. I also have illustrations of the action scenes. I do some fifty to seventy-five rough sketches, and later my art director comes in for what we call "the kill." He will finish it off for me. That's how I start to make a movie.

I can be very objective this way. You write on your typewriter in your room, you read it aloud to people, you read it for yourself and it reads good, and you think you're a genius. And your friends and the actors read it, and the actors say, "Isn't it wonderful?" Especially if the parts are good for them. But the blackboard never lies. If I see that your character is in the middle of the first column and then later on near the end of the second column, I know there is something wrong. Maybe I could take you out, and tell the story without you. That's what I mean by objective.

I work on the set with a designer, with the wardrobe people, everybody. I rehearse, minimum a week, with the actors. And I rehearse in that week at least two days with my whole crew. And we shoot every key scene in the picture without film. The last day of rehearsal we shoot the toughest scene without film. Let's say it's Friday. The cast all go home at six o'clock. They rest over the weekend. Monday we repeat that scene. The actors are acclimatized now. They're well rehearsed. They know exactly what to do. It gives me a chance to introduce new business.

For instance, I have an actor who has to sit down at a table and pour himself a glass of water. For one week I will rehearse him pouring that glass of water. And he says a certain line, say, "I like Stockholm." And he knows that when he says that line, he must pour himself water. Now Monday without his knowing it I change that glass of water to another part of the set. I move props around. Now when he says, "I like Stockholm," there's realism in his face, because he's really looking for the water. As he looks around, I catch a look that's new. And that's what I do right through the whole picture. And they never know, whenever they are to shoot a scene, when any business is added. I am liable to rehearse them, rehearse them, rehearse them, and suddenly in the actual take, when I want a little surprise, I will have an actor who is not in the scene just step right in. He'll say something. Or I'll say something like, "When you act, why don't you wear shoes?" And they look around silly. And I use that shot for something else.

I use a gun a lot. I put a gun under the lens and actors don't know it. When I shoot that gun, I get an expression out of an actor's face that's beautiful.

And I also use a gun when I want to cue my people. If I have a street scene, it is very difficult to depend on walkie-talkies, handkerchief-waving, or a whistle. If you have three or four things happening simultaneously and everybody knows that their cue is a gunshot, they laugh at it, but it comes in handy.

SB: Do you let your actors improvise too?
SF: No, I won't gamble on that, because they might improvise some-

thing which doesn't belong to the character. No, no. Many directors do that, but I won't.

I Shot Jesse James

SB: You started your directorial career with a Western, *I Shot Jesse James*, which looked a bit different from other Westerns from that time.

SF: Well, the New York papers tagged a new word to it—which I laughed at—they used the expression that for the first time they'd seen an "adult" Western. Because no one is on a horse and there is just one quick chase, not really a chase, just one man going from one house to another.

I made one error. I used a saloon. In westerns to come I will not use a saloon, unless it is essential to the story. Every western has a saloon, where they're always gambling. They never wash, they never eat, they never work, no one ever knows where they get their money. And even if you come in there at ten o'clock in the morning, there is a floor show with a girl singing. As long as there is a western, they'll have a saloon where there's a girl with a golden heart.

I made *I Shot Jesse James* because I am interested in assassinations. And I am interested in what makes an assassin act. So I picked the man who killed one of the most despicable, ruthless, falsely publicized characters in the American western folklore, Jesse Woodson James, a true bastard. He was so low that his first job was to rob a train with his brother, and the train was a hospital train filled with wounded soldiers. They killed all the wounded soldiers and took the few dollars. He and his brother were two illiterate, uncouth rats. They were fifteen and seventeen years old when they joined Quantrill's Raiders, during the Civil War. Jesse James at fifteen was assigned a job by Quantrill: he would masquerade as a girl, pick up soldiers and bring them into a house called the House of Joy, a house of prostitution. He would get drunk with the soldiers—he had a very pretty face—and when they all got drunk, he and Quantrill would kill the soldiers and rob them.

That was Jesse James. In case we ever meet after I die, I will hit him as soon as I see him. He was no good. But thanks to many pop-magazine writers, he was celebrated and, over a period of years, he became a hero.

So I wanted to do the story of a man who kills another man. My story was based on one quote from Oscar Wilde: "Each man kills the thing he loves." We find out that in the end of the story, the assassin loves the victim. No homosexuality. But the last line in the thing is that he says, "I love you."

SB: *I Shot Jesse James* was built up from a ballad, wasn't it?

SF: "The Ballad of Jesse James." It's a very famous ballad, and I use that melody for the main musical theme of the picture. The ballad is about Robert Ford, who killed Jesse James. And I got an idea about how to use this ballad. I'd have a troubadour, a traveling singer, come into a saloon and sing a song about the man who killed Jesse James. And in the song he's no good, Robert Ford, the assassin: ". . . the dirty little coward who shot Mr. Howard in the back . . ." Suddenly one of the men in the bar (it's the first time this kind of thing is used, this kind of drama with a ballad) says, "I'm Robert Ford." Now the man stops singing. Ford says, "Sing it!" The man says, "Well, I don't think it's a very popular song, Mr. Ford." But Ford repeats, "Sing it!" So the man has to sing the song to the man it's about, and he insults him with the lyrics. The singer almost dies doing that. You see sweat coming down his face. Afterwards, my idea was stolen for I don't know how many westerns.

Run of the Arrow

SF: It was the first American picture where the Indians won, and I was invited by the Indian Commissioner to Washington. He ran the picture for all the senators, including from North Dakota and South Dakota and Wyoming. Then the Indians wrote me and invited me to go to their tribes. And they liked the movie, because they didn't act like, "Ugh! Me go. White man speak broken tongue. Red man speak straight tongue." You see, I wanted to keep away from that. But that started a little thing; friends of mine who make pictures said, "We'll make pictures, too, showing the Indians won."

You know, the Sioux nation is the only nation within the territory of the United States that was never defeated by the United States.

SB: The Confederacy was defeated.

SF: In *Run of the Arrow* I tried to get a symbolism of the feeling of the South in 1865. I can appreciate and even accept a sore loser. It's a natural thing that when you're in a fight and you lose, you're sore. You get unhappy. That's OK. However I don't think it's normal for you to maintain that childish mood of being sore for over seventy-five years. I wanted to show that there was no change in the United States in the Southern parts from 1865 to when I made the picture in 1957. No change whatsoever. They still fly the Confederate flag down there. We, up in the North, are still called "damn Yankees." They have an alibi why they lost. And the feeling of hate, instead of decreasing has increased. That's the reason for the ending of my picture. I wrote that only "you" can write the end of the story. And I meant the Southern people. I hope they left that in.

SB: Yes, they did. What was taken out were the more violent bits, for instance the scene where [Lieutenant Driscoll] Ralph Meeker is being dragged after the horses.

SF: Oh, did they take that out? And the emasculation? It was a very striking scene and it shocked the people, though I didn't show the real thing. The reason I didn't show the real thing is that Meeker got so excited and said to me, "Now wait a minute, who's gonna handle the knife?" And I said, "I am." And that's what he was afraid of. He said, "Now don't let it slip. My girl is waiting for me for dinner." He was really concerned. Because I get carried away. You see, I don't care if I do anything wrong, if it was an accident. I don't care. *Je me'n moque!*

I thought it would be time to show the truth that in many of the battles the Indians—particularly the Sioux—did not massacre all people (I did a lot of research for this) and often sent back survivors with a message, "Don't make trouble!" They often did that. And I was very fed up with many American movies where Indians are jumping around and yelling and screaming and killing. The only ones who used to do that in the old days were the beatniks of the Indians, the avant-garde of the Indians, the delinquents.

Forty Guns

SB: I very much liked the ballad scenes in *Forty Guns*.

SF: That young man who is singing the song in the picture is not an actor. He is what we call a professional record-seller. If you wrote a song and you wanted it for Crosby or Sinatra, this man would do a record of your song and sing it the way Sinatra sings it. Then the song is sent to Sinatra and generally he buys it, because this man is an expert. He can sing like any singer. But in *Forty Guns* he sang the way he himself sang. But nobody cared about him, because he has no name. "Jidge" Carroll is his name.

In that scene I had no saloon. I had nobody chasing anybody on a horse. There is no gun shooting until the very end of the picture, really gun shooting. There are no barroom brawls and things like that.

SB: A very beautiful scene in the picture is the burial, which is staged in one long take.

SF: I've seen ten thousand funeral scenes. I'd love a funeral scene in the rain but I could not use one because somebody used it already. It is quite difficult to dig a grave in the rain—there's the water, and the earth keeps sliding in again. So I thought it would be very effective if we got black horses, a black hearse, a glass hearse. And only the widow is at the funeral. It's one of my favorite scenes: just two horses, two people, and a wagon. It was shot very fast.

The original title of the picture was *A Woman with a Whip*, like the song in the picture. But I didn't want to use that title, because I'd heard that a book had just come out about the life of Eva Peron, and it was called *The Lady with a Whip*, or something like that.

The Crimson Kimono

SF: My favorite scene in *The Crimson Kimono* is the scene where the detective and the girl come out from the police headquarters and go into a Chinese restaurant to sit down with the old lady, the artist. I am very proud of that scene because it is a very tough scene. I had a long shot as they come across the street, and I pulled back into a real Chinese restaurant. They went through the restaurant, went into a corner, where I sat them in a booth. Now the restaurant was very narrow, and we could not get the camera in. And the booth was still more narrow, very small. So I had them take all the stools out. Unscrew them and take out the pedestals. Now I had room for the dolly, but I didn't have room for the operator. So he had to slide on his derrière along the counter. But as he began to slide along the counter, there was friction with his pants and the camera jerked. So I said, "Let's put some oil on him." Then he told me he could not go home with his oily pants to his wife. But I said, "I don't care. That's your fault getting married." We did that several times and then the shot was smooth. That was a good shot. I like shots like that!

But my favorite shots . . . I have two favorites. One is in *Park Row*. I open up in a saloon, 1886, and a fight starts. The men come out from the saloon into the street. They fight down the street. They upset different people. And the first man defeats the second man. He goes into an office and has a big scene with a woman in there, shakes her up a little bit, comes out, walks down a block, goes behind a big statue of Benjamin Franklin, and goes into the *third* set. Now that scene was taken without a cut. I had to have a little mike planted on my actor. And I had to strap the operator to the camera. In the first trial, the camera whipped around and the men flew in all directions. It was like a roller coaster. A good shot.

The other shot I like is in *Forty Guns*. It opens up in a bedroom with one of the brothers talking. He comes out from the bedroom, walks down the stairs, and meets the other brother. They start to walk. They meet the sheriff. They walk four blocks. They go to the telegraph office, send a telegram. Barbara Stanwyck passes them with the forty horsemen, and then they walk past the camera. That is the longest dolly shot in Hollywood.

You know what's bad about that? It's very dangerous. When you build a long dolly, a track as you know, it sags. The longer it gets, the saggier it becomes. And I don't want the feeling that we're going down a mountain. I want it straight. I think the trick is to get very short planks.

SB: In the striptease scenes in *Shock Corridor* and *The Crimson Kimono* you never see the public, though you can sense it's there.

SF: First of all, this economically saves a lot of money. Secondly, let's say we have the money to spend. I think it's a bore to cut to people watching an act, to cut to baldheaded men, to cut to fellows with mouths open—shots, we call them artistic shots—five or six cuts. You've seen that a thousand times. I think to myself—I may be wrong—this is a more effective way of shooting it. And actually I want to see the girl!

The Crimson Kimono caused a lot of trouble. It was difficult in the beginning for the people financing the picture to accept the idea—not that they cared, but they knew that a lot of theatre owners did—that a Japanese man not only ends up with a white woman but also outrivals a white man, who is a nice guy, too. But I have to give Columbia credit for financing it, because this is a very ticklish subject in the United States. There's no law against it, but it's even worse sometimes than if there were a law. It's an unspoken law.

Underworld U.S.A.

SF: I didn't even know I was going to do this picture. Humphrey Bogart bought a serial from the *Saturday Evening Post* called "Underworld U.S.A.," a documentary report about prohibition written by a Boston newspaperman, Joseph Dineen. Bogart died. His estate, Santana, owned it. [Producer] Ray Stark bought the serial from the Santana estate for

85,000 bucks. He couldn't do anything with it because nobody cared about bootleggers. I was asked by the Studio if I would make a picture with that title. Ray Stark would get back his $85,000, and I said OK.

I had more trouble with that script than with any other script. Because I got all the information, the narcotics figures, the profit figures, gambling figures, prostitution figures, I had them in the script, then I had to take them out. I'd got the actual figures from Washington. That was censored. But the censors were right in a way. The average young fellow, fifteen, seventeen, eighteen, seeing the picture and *listening* to the figures would say, "What the hell, why should I work hard? I mean these men are making billions a year, not millions!" The censors said, "You take fifty or a hundred thousand young men and they'll say, 'What the heck, if I could make just a hundred thousand that way, it's good enough for me.'"

SB: You had Shakespeare in mind while writing *Underworld U.S.A.*?
SF: I love him. He used one plot, and once he knew it's successful, he used it over and over again. He was guilty of James Bond. And the reason why his plot was successful is that it was honest emotion. Somebody is jealous of someone, or somebody wants to double-cross someone, or somebody is greedy. He couldn't go wrong with any of that. It's funny but I have not heard this connection with Shakespeare brought up before. The only one who mentioned that was me with Mr. [Sam] Briskin, who was in charge of Columbia. I mentioned Hamlet and also Edmond Dantes. I didn't want to keep those a secret. I even had a line in the script about *The Count of Monte Cristo*. The little woman says, "How can you carry such a grudge?" I even had one of the characters reading the book.

SB: Do you prefer working in color or black-and-white?
SF: I don't believe in the argument that certain stories lend themselves to color. If you made a movie and it was a damn good drama, frankly I didn't care whether it's in color or not. We've accepted the idea that certain serious, intimate subjects should only be in black-and-white.

SB: In the minor parts you often use the same actors.
SF: I have to. They're my friends. They hang around, they wait for me to make a picture. Every time I finish a picture, I make an announcement through a mike that from now on, and in the next picture, I don't want to use them, I don't like them, I don't want to see them, and I hate them. And then I start writing a new one, and they come around asking me

what I'm writing, and they hang around, and before you know it I say, "All right!" I've used some of them for years.

SB: Actors like Neyle Morrow and Paul Dubov?
SF: They're in everything, and Gerald Milton I use. He left the business and has an investment brokerage company. He's one of the most successful brokers in Los Angeles. But whenever I make a picture, he calls, and he leaves his sixty or seventy employees and acts for me. In my last picture, *The Naked Kiss*, all I wanted was a big man. A prostitute in a bar comes over and hits him. That's Gerald Milton. But all these actor friends, they are dependable, they are good. They know how I work. And they all claim it will bring bad luck if I don't hire them.

SB: You often use long takes in your films. Do you prefer working with actors and on the set that way?
SF: I like it for one reason especially. After five or six minutes, you can tell the difference in an actor's voice. There's something about it that to me is real, and you can't get this feeling with speeches, cut, new angle, speeches, cut. Put together, it always has a funny sound to it. Actors become more tense, revitalized, when it's a long take. They're afraid if they make an error, they'll spoil the whole scene.

I am going to be an actor! In a few days, I'll meet the director and discuss the part. It's a part of a couple of minutes. It's for fun. The director's name is Godard. He wants me to play a Hollywood director, I guess. He did this once before with Fritz Lang. So for the first time in my life, I'm going to feel like a little starlet. And I'm going to act like one. Someone told me, but I don't know if this is authentic, that it's an orgy with some forty girls in it. If this is true, I'm very, very excited.

Samuel Fuller

Eric Sherman and Martin Rubin/1968

From *The Director's Event: Interviews with Five American Film-Makers* (New York: Atheneum Books, 1970). Reprinted by permission of Eric Sherman and Martin Rubin.

Eric Sherman and I were two enthusiastic but inexperienced undergraduates when we interviewed Samuel Fuller at his home in Los Angeles in November 1968. Sam and his lovely wife Christa graciously invited us over for dinner first. After much wine and conversation, the interview did not commence until nearly midnight. Sam frequently addressed one or the other of us as "lad," and he seemed to take a sly delight in plying us with Cuban cigars and high-proof Polish vodka. The shot glasses would be quickly refilled after the merest sip, with the encouragement to drink up. Eventually one of the interviewers passed out, but Sam was indefatigable: "What's the matter, lad? Are you tired? I'm not tired! Got any more questions?" At around 3 a.m., he took pity on us, and we returned to complete the interview a day or two later. Such was the force field of Sam's personality that, for several days after the interview, Eric and I found ourselves speaking with Fulleresque inflections and using his distinct brand of slang ("loot" for "money," "boff" for "fuck," "gibble-gabble" for "nonsense").

Even to such newcomers as me and Eric, it quickly became obvious that only a few micromillimeters beneath Sam's flamboyant tough-guy manner lay a great deal of sweetness and warmth. It perhaps took a little longer to discern that his Runyonesque persona fronted a very learned and sensitive artist, with dimensions (his Jewishness, for instance) that had been barely touched upon in his films, writings, or interviews. I think that Eric and I were lucky to catch Sam speaking so directly and substantially about his art, with less of the "playing-the-character-of-

Sam-Fuller" that dominates other interviews I have read or heard. Perhaps it was the late hour, perhaps it was the Polish vodka, or perhaps he was just being generous to a couple of green lads from Yale.
—*Martin Rubin*

I Shot Jesse James

Q: In *I Shot Jesse James*, the Robert Ford character [John Ireland] strikes one at first as a rat. But as the film progresses, he seems to become more sympathetic.
A: I'll make it very brief about Mr. Robert Ford. I happen to like Robert Ford, because he did something which should have been done quite a bit earlier in the life of Jesse Woodson James. Jesse James was a half-assed homo who impersonated a girl for Quantrill's Raiders when he was fifteen. Acting as a hooker, he enticed soldiers into a little shack called "The House of Love," where these bastard raiders robbed the soldiers and killed them. When he was eighteen, Jesse and his brother held up a hospital train, wherein they robbed all the casualties and killed them.

Since I despise Mr. James (and would give my right eyeball to make the true story of Jesse James), I've always had sympathy for Robert Ford. One day, the real story of Jesse James will be made. It will shock people. Rough! Vicious! We have young squirts today who are supposed to be under the spell of narcotics, and they hold up banks and mug women. They're cream puffs compared with these old guys. They knocked off people immediately.

Q: In your picture, how well do you think Robert Ford understood his own motives when he kills Jesse?
A: Oh, he knew he'd get amnesty. He had to make a selection between freedom, a couple of dollars, a woman, and a little farm—and his friend [Jesse]. Being human, Ford naturally decided that the sacrificial lamb was the friend. Oh, he understood it all right. What he didn't understand, until the end of the picture, was that he walked in a daze. I tried to get a groping, not half-witted, but not too mentally alert type of a man. The last line in the picture is my [version of the] story. Ford says to the girl, "I'll tell you something I haven't told anyone. I'm sorry I killed Jesse. I loved him." I wanted that type of an association. Robert Lippert, the man who financed the picture, didn't catch that. He just thought it was a kind of Damon-Pythias relationship, and he let it remain.

Q: How much were you relying on popular knowledge of the shooting of Jesse James? In Jesse's living room in the movie, the picture on the wall is tilted. Would the audience know the popular version of Jesse's death, and respond to that?

A: Even as kids, we've all seen illustrations of Jesse being shot while adjusting a picture on the wall. I wanted to get a simplification of what we know, but I wanted it to be fresh. I tried to get the feeling of a gun and a weird room by tilting the camera. I wanted the camera to tilt slightly in one direction and the picture to tilt in another. So that when it evens out, we have death. I wanted something weird in the beginning, but when it's over, dead men are usually horizontal, and everything is simple, on one line.

I love the West. I read a lot about the West, and I'm shocked, I'm ashamed that in pictures they have not made the true story of the winning of the West—comprising 90 percent foreigners, 100 percent laborers, nothing to do with guns. Streets, mountains, roads, bridges, streams, forests—that's the winning of the West to me. Hard! Tremendous, tremendous fight. But we have, as you know [instead], cowboys and Indians and all that. Shane comes into town, cleans it up, and leaves. He's doing that every week now on TV.

That's why I didn't want any horsemanship in the picture. After we finished shooting, Lippert put in some stock shots of people riding around. I didn't want that. I'm not interested in a horse story. I'm not even interested in Jesse. I'm interested in Ford, and how difficult it must be for an assassin to kill someone, especially someone he knows. How difficult!

The Steel Helmet

A: I made *The Steel Helmet* in ten days. Ten days! One set. One-half a day with all the action at Griffith Park. Twenty-five university students as extras. [Only] twenty-five men! We couldn't afford anything else. I made them look like 350 or 400. Sometimes, when you can't afford it, you improvise, and it comes off better.

Q: The relation between Sergeant Zack and the little boy in *The Steel Helmet* is similar to the one between Price and Drew in *The Baron of Arizona*. Zack doesn't realize the boy's attachment to him until after the boy is killed . . .

A: Ah yes! I see what you mean. Any damn emotional cementing between them grows on them. Yes, you're right. What Zack epitomized there was the symbol of a non-com: no emotion whatsoever. None! Because if you have emotions, you're not in war. There's no time for emotion. It becomes a job. You wake up. You work a little. Maybe you go on a patrol or a little skirmish line. Your fight is very brief. You rest. You crap. You eat. Then you go out and shoot again. You go to sleep. Then you get up . . .

If you do this for three years, it's just a job. It's a tremendous machine inside you. The only emotion you have is: "When do I get out of here, and when does somebody replace me?" That's the only emotion you experience in war. You become aware of sounds. You become aware of sight. And you become aware of trust in man. Very aware. If I know you two fellows are on my right, that's fine. If I'm worried about you, I'm in trouble.

So I thought it might be a very effective scene if Zack blows his top, not because of the enemy or shooting or all that, but because of a kid. You should never blow your top over a person who's on your side. The kid was on his side. You did catch something there; it was a growing love affair. It was a love story.

When Zack blew his top, he shot down an unarmed POW. To me, that was not a shocker. But it was to the press. Tremendous shocker. A lot of editorials. I have all the newspapers. Big full-page interviews asking, "WOULD YOU SHOOT THIS MAN?" You see, I think it's a little stupid, when you're in war, to hold your fire just because a man puts his hands up. Five minutes before that, he's shooting at you. He runs out of ammunition; he can put his hands up. I mean, certainly there's no law. If there's a law in war, then we're really completely nuts. Now, we're only 99 percent nuts. But if there's a law. . . . How can there be a law for an illegal act?

So, I cannot get concerned about shooting a prisoner. It means nothing to me. Absolutely nothing. I think the idea of shooting a *man* is more important. I don't care whether he's a friend or an enemy. But the idea that we have laws and Geneva Conventions and rules and regulations is a cover up for a lot of stupid things.

Q: Why did you give such emphasis to the Buddha monument in the film?

A: I specifically wanted to put the blood plasma in the palm of the Buddha. I wanted to show the blood running out of his hand into the Commie. I thought it would be very touching to have death there in the lap of *his* God, and within minutes that the whole temple is going to be obliterated. But still that Buddha remains.

The big Buddha in Kamakura, Japan, was surrounded by a tremendous temple. Many hundreds of years ago, there was a quake. Everything was demolished except this Buddha. . . . Oh! You saw it in *House of Bamboo*. That's the Kamakura Buddha. I did know the story of that Buddha, and I thought it was strange that it remained. Just like the Greek relics today. I don't know why in the hell certain columns remain and certain ones don't. That's the flavor I tried to get with the Buddha in *The Steel Helmet*.

Q: At the end of the film, after the major attack on the temple, the three survivors are all outcasts in some way—the Negro, the Oriental, and the bald-headed fellow. This adds a very downbeat note to the "victory" over the North Koreans.
A: I deliberately put a line in that scene which is strictly dogface dialogue. No matter what happens, when the battle is over, there's always one man who's going to say, "I'm hungry." And there's always one fellow who's ready to vomit. But the theme of *The Steel Helmet* is the ending. That's what I wanted to show: that this was *not* the end. Wars go on and on and on. There's no end to the story.

Fixed Bayonets

A: In *Fixed Bayonets* I wanted to do the story of a fellow [Richard Basehart] who cannot knock off an enemy soldier. In the end, when he does—out of pure fear, panic, frustration, and lack of coordination—they compliment him, and he accepts the compliment. That's what happens in war.

To me, the thrill of war—and there is a tremendous thrill—is death. That's the thing I'm really interested in, because it's the only mystery. That's why I'll always dramatize it. I don't think anything is more dramatic in motion pictures than death, even though we assume we're coldblooded and can take it for granted. I don't know of any other subject.

[In the War,] I seldom heard a dying man make a speech. The general things you heard, when a man was hit next to you: "Oh, no. Oh, hell. Oh, hell, no. Ooooh noooo. Please. Please. Not me!"

Q: That's what the "mute" soldier in *The Steel Helmet* says when he's killed.
A: Oh right! That's what he says. That's what you say, and you go. It's selfish. All exits are selfish—and personal. And that's the way it should be.

Q: The battle scenes in *Fixed Bayonets* are impressive and quite unusual: quick cuts, no sense of space or broad spectacle, very realistic and terrifying.

A: Very intimate, right. First of all, I had a tremendous ice machine. The set was built, and I rehearsed the actors and the stuntmen. Then I was ready to go. I told everybody, "Just leave the stage. Get a little air. Relax." Then I said, "Ice it!" That big hose just went whoosshh, and the whole set was ice. Then I called the actors back in. Were they surprised! Those falls, there's no acting in them. Didn't you get a feeling of panic? It was real. They were slipping all over the place. They knew there were explosions going on, and they had to get out of there.

That reminds me of a funny incident on *Fixed Bayonets*. One of our stuntmen was hurt. Nothing serious, he twisted his leg. I found out that when stuntmen are hurt and taken off a picture, their salary is stopped. So I got an idea. I told my assistant, "Use him as a casualty." Well, by the end of the week, I had a casualty list this long! Anyone who was hurt continued in the picture as a casualty. Only, they were real casualties! If a fellow couldn't walk in the picture, he really couldn't walk.

Q: I liked the scene at the beginning of the picture where all the troops are pulling out, and the rear-guard platoon is left behind. They're standing there, frozen, while a very distorted, muffled melody is heard on the soundtrack.

A: I wanted a combination of "On the Banks of the Wabash" and "Taps." I thought that was a touching melody for the scene. I was very anxious to get the effect of a rear guard: the abandonment.

Q: In that scene, when the troops pull out, you track across the faces of the men in the rear guard. When they cross the river at the end, their faces all pass by the camera, and they look almost the same as at the beginning. Their situation is the same.

A: Did you get the sense of balance there? All except the ones who didn't make it.

Pickup on South Street

Q: The opening of *Pickup on South Street*—when Richard Widmark picks the girl's pocketbook containing the secret information—is played without dialogue. This gives the action a great deal of ambiguity. It's only much later that you find out what actually transpired. So, instead of the

"Commies vs. the Good Guys," you're concerned with personal issues from the start.

A: You're right about the ambiguity. The ending is like that, too. Some people thought, "Well, I guess Widmark'll go off with the girl and be happy." I gave her a line at the end to show that they'll never change. The cop says, "No matter what happens, I'll find this son of a bitch in a week or two with his hand in somebody's pocket." She says, "You wanna bet?" The way she said that showed that I wanted the audience to feel he eventually will go back to picking pockets, and she'll go back to doing whatever the hell she was doing.

This is what I got a kick out of in the picture: the idea of having a pickpocket, a police informer, and a half-assed hooker as the three main characters. The picture was made in about eighteen or twenty days at Fox. A big picture for me. The whole thing was shot in downtown L.A., and I used a lot of tricks to make it look like New York.

Q: Although you establish the city very forcefully in the film, you seem to be more interested in individuals than in the structures, political or otherwise, which surround the characters.

A: That's why I played down the political situation in *Pickup*. I was not interested in the structure. I could have had a hell of a big scene, with fifty or sixty extras. They're all gathered together, and the head man says, "This is terrible. What about the [Communist] Party?" You never hear the word "Party" in my film.

You are never even told that the FBI man in *Pickup* is from the FBI. He's just from the government. I didn't want to pinpoint it. Just before I made the picture, [Klaus] Fuchs, the British espionage agent, had been arrested for selling information to Russia. The government man in the film says to Widmark, "You know about Fuchs. You know what he did." Widmark says, "I don't know what you're talking about. I don't care."

Q: This seemed to be the most "close-up" of your films. You even kept dollying in from a close-up to a more extreme close-up.

A: Oh, yes. You noticed that? I like to do that sometimes. *Jesse James* was also shot with a lot of close-ups because I'm not interested in the bank or the people in the bank. I'm interested in a teller who is going to be shot and the man who is going to shoot him. The same thing in *Pickup*. Come to think of it, [there were] very few extras are in the film, very few people around.

Q: I especially liked was the way you moved the camera.
A: If your camera is moving, and your action is moving—boy, you have action! If your action is moving, and your camera is stationary, it is not that effective. It's also better not to just follow the action. Again, it's your eye. I want to go beyond the eye. So you have two sets of eyes: the camera is moving, and your own eye is moving.

Q: Just before the scene of Thelma Ritter's death, there's a shot of her selling her neckties in a construction area at night. I got a hellish, underworld feeling from that shot. Were you trying for this?
A: Oh, no. I wanted something that is being born right before somebody is dead. I wanted something *alive*. I wanted one of those riveting machines and fire and lights and life. Alive! Noisy! Because it's going to be very quiet soon—for her.

Q: Just as a footnote, I'd like to ask about one of my favorite bit characters: Lightnin' Louie.
A: Lightnin' Louie was played by a card expert and magician from Chicago named Victor Perry. It was his first and last picture. I just happened to meet him. I asked him, "Are you good with your hands?" He said, "Am I good? Just watch my act!" I said, "What I want in my film is a man who is so indifferent to people that he has contempt even for the people he's selling information to—especially if they interfere with him while he's eating. That's why I want a man like you, with a big belly. Now let me see you pick up some money with the chopsticks and just keep eating with them." Did you like that touch? That's exactly why I used him.

House of Bamboo

A: *House of Bamboo* was the first American picture made in Japan, and the first time I really went on location.

Q: The pre-credits sequence—the train holdup and the murder in the shadow of Mt. Fujiyama—was very striking.
A: I didn't want to show Mt. Fuji as you always see it—with the cherry blossoms. I wanted white against white against white. In the foreground, I wanted that *black* train. I wanted a flavor of grim bleakness. Then, as we pulled away from death, the murder of the soldier, you saw a woman running. The titles came on, and we started getting lush with color, little

by little. By the time she's reporting to the police, we were in color! That excited me.

Q: Like *Steel Helmet, House of Bamboo* is essentially a love story between two men, Robert Stack and Robert Ryan.
A: Definitely. That's epitomized by one line of dialogue that I gave Ryan. It comes right after the first robbery. Ryan is trying to figure out why, in Stack's case, he [Ryan] broke his gang's policy of killing wounded men so that they won't talk to the police. First, he says to Stack, "I don't know why I saved your neck." Then he turns to the other men and says, "Will anyone please tell me why I did it?"

That's the big line, the cementing between them. I hoped it would get people a little nervous, because it's usually a line that a man says about a woman: "Why did I marry her? What am I doing with her? Why did I go out with her? Will anyone please tell me why I did it?" That's as close as I could get to it, when Ryan says that line.

Q: The way in which we judge these two characters is typical of your films. On a structural, institutional level, Stack is a police agent out to stop a crime wave, and we should sympathize with him. But on a more personal level—the male love story—Ryan is more sympathetic.
A: I told Ryan to never say "my father" but to say "pappy." Right away, you have to like any guy who says "pappy," because he likes his father. When Stack talked about his family, he was dull. After all, he's just a cop. Just a cop from California. Didn't mean a thing.

Q: The way Ryan ran his crime syndicate was fascinating. A robbery was conducted like a military maneuver, with battle maps, briefing sessions, reconnaissance, photographs.
A: After the War, I tried to sell Metro a story about a group of men who were in the same platoon, and when the War is over, they form a combination of criminals. They take Fort Knox, using the same military maneuver with which they knocked out a pillbox on Omaha Beach. The studio didn't buy it. So when I was asked to do *House of Bamboo*, I figured I'd use that situation.

Run of the Arrow

A: I wanted Rod Steiger to play the lead because he didn't look like a typical American hero. He was blubbery. I thought he would look ungainly on a horse, and he did. He was perfect for that role; he was a misfit.

The Steiger character became a religious zealot as far as hatred was concerned. He acted the same way the losers act in any war, in this case the
Confederates.

Q: You often use a prop as more than just a symbol or a motif, but almost
as a character, such as the helmet in *Steel Helmet* and the bullet in *Run of
the Arrow*.
A: Yes. My original title for the film was *The Last Bullet*. That's what started me thinking about the whole story: what happened to the last car-
tridge fired in the Civil War? I thought it was a good title, but it sounded
too much like a Western.

Q: In this film and in *Forty Guns*, you used a lot of very slow dissolves.
Why?
A: That was for the mood. I tried to time each one of those dissolves so
that it was almost like music, a beautiful piece of music, and I had all hell
break loose right after or right before that. I couldn't have gotten any
other contrast unless I used a long talking scene, and I didn't want that.

Q: Why did you concentrate on feet rather than faces in the "Run of the
Arrow" scene?
A: I shot that scene without my star. Steiger sprained his ankle right before we shot it, and he was taken off to the hospital. I used a young Indian in his place. Nobody noticed it. They thought I was being highly
creative, highly artistic: "Imagine! Almost a boy wonder, a genius! Sensational! The way he shot it by just showing the feet!" Well, I would have
shot about 80 percent of the scene with just feet anyway, because that's
the whole idea of the Run. But occasionally I would have liked to whip
up with the camera and show Steiger's face, just as I did with [Jay C.] Flip-
pen. I couldn't, because he was in the hospital.

Joe Biroc, the cameraman, did a terrific job on that scene. There are a
couple of shots of two little dots in the distance; it's the Indian running
after Steiger. I don't know how Biroc caught that, but it was exactly what
I wanted: you have to look for a moment before you notice them, because
it's all vivid color, and then you see one speck chasing another speck.

China Gate

Q: I like the scene where Angie Dickinson leaves [Lee] Van Cleef and
blows up the ammo dump, thus killing herself. It's done so quickly. She
never stops to think, "What am I doing?" She just does it, because she

has to. These types of decisions are found frequently in your films—for example, in *Underworld U.S.A.*, when Tolly Devlin kills Boss Connors, and in *The Naked Kiss*, when Kelly kills Grant.

A: If it's anything connected with death, it should be quick, unless you have a good dramatic reason for stalling—for example, in *Underworld U.S.A.*, when [Cliff] Robertson goes to kill Paul Dubov. I didn't mind the stalling there, because first of all he's going to maneuver the death of this man; second, he's going to torture him; and third, he's not going to shoot him himself. But if Robertson were going to commit the act personally, I'd have him blow Dubov's head off as soon as he walks in the door. It's very hard for me to accept a lot of gibble-gabble before a shooting. Instead, I want *impact*.

When I told Angie to run through that cave, I conceived the whole thing as taking place in five seconds or less, from the beginning of the run to the blow-up. Because not only is time important, but if she *walked* there, we would fall into a dangerous category: now she's going to deliberate. She would be hesitant, and she shouldn't be hesitant. It's like a suicide. If you're going to kill yourself, kill yourself. Don't call the police and your mother and your father and your uncle. But you hit on something that's very close to me: the *rapidity*. Didn't that scene shock you a little?

Forty Guns

A: I don't like the title *Forty Guns*; it's meaningless to me. I was going to call it *Woman with a Whip*. Originally, Marilyn Monroe wanted to play the lead role. She liked the idea of this girl surrounded by all these men. I thought she was too young for what I wanted. I wanted a mother-sister flavor there.

The stuntmen refused to do the scene where the Stanwyck character is dragged by a horse. They thought it was too dangerous. But Stanwyck said she'd do it, and she did it. We did it the first time, and I said, "I didn't like it. It was too far away from the camera truck. We're not getting what I want." So we tried it again, and I didn't like it. She made no complaint. We tried it a third time, and it was just the way I wanted it. She was quite bruised.

Q: There is a pervasive sense of death in the picture, connected with sexual acts specifically. The most striking example of this is the wedding scene, where the groom is shot and falls dead on his bride.

A: I liked the idea of the honeymoon bed being the grave. The only time he really got to touch her, he was dead. I thought I would even contrast that scene a little bit, as far as sex was concerned, with the scene where the gunsmith's daughter measures [Gene] Barry for a weapon. I thought I'd have a little fun with sex, because the connotations were all there. I had a shot where he looks at the girl through a loose gun barrel, and as she walks, he pans with her, just like a camera. When I was in Paris, Godard told me he used that shot in *Breathless*, except that instead of a rifle, [Jean-Paul] Belmondo rolls up a newspaper and follows [Jean] Seberg when she's walking around his room.

I couldn't use my original ending. I was asked to change it, and I changed it. The ending I originally shot was powerful. I had [Barry] Sullivan facing the killer, the young brother of Stanwyck. I had him grab Stanwyck and hold her in front of him. He knew he had Sullivan in a spot. I had him defy Sullivan. And Sullivan kills Stanwyck. Then he kills the boy and walks away. That was the end of the picture.

I had to put in that line where Sullivan says that he aimed the bullet so that it wouldn't kill Stanwyck. She's alive in the end, and they're happy. I didn't like that ending. A lot of people liked it, because they like to see the boy and the girl get together. I don't think that's important. I think it's much more dramatic the other way, because Sullivan has to blow his top. That's why he hasn't used a gun in ten years. But the moment he squeezes that trigger, he's a different man. He's an executioner, and he kills anything in front of him. It's a rough ending.

I've seen so many pictures, from *High Noon* back, where the heavy grabs the girl and holds her in front of him, putting the hero in a hell of an embarrassing situation. Always, at the last minute, she pushes him away, and the hero kills him. I don't like that in any Western. It doesn't make sense.

Verboten!

Q: *Verboten!* seems to be your most chaotic film. Every scene was done in a different style. For example, documentary footage was intercut with a street set, and film-clip montages intermingled with long takes. What linked these scenes was that nearly every one dealt with a form of hysteria.

A: I'm very glad that you brought that up. I used the contrasts in shooting to help maintain chaos, because I'm very touchy about that subject, about postwar Germany. I had a very good ending, but I was forced to change it. I had the American soldier shot at the end. I had him killed by an MP, another American soldier, who saw this fellow walking around by the fire and shot him because he was dressed as a civilian. The other soldiers come over and say, "Who is it?" The MP turns the body over with his foot, and he says, "Ah hell, another Kraut." Not that I want every hero to die. In this case, I thought it would give me more impact.

But I'm very close to the subject of *Verboten!* During the war we had a lot of arguments over whether there is a difference between a German and a Nazi. With the exception of one experience I had, I did not meet a single German, from the day we invaded Germany to the end of the war in Czechoslovakia, who said he was a Nazi. The one exception was a fifteen- or sixteen-year-old girl in a little town outside of Aachen. I was on a patrol with several men, and we asked her for water. She told us to get our asses away from there. We even tried to impress on her that behind us was the First U.S. Infantry Division of twelve thousand men. It meant nothing to her. That's the only German I ever met who told us she was a Nazi and told us to go to hell. I'll never forget that. Everyone else said, "I don't know what's going on." Just like the Southerner in *Run of the Arrow*. You know; it's always the other fellow.

I was very touchy about that. I took a lot of footage during the war. Not just good stuff. Great stuff. My stuff. Stuff you don't see in the Army Pictorial Service films.

The last battle of World War II was in Falkenau, Czechoslovakia. The town was near a concentration camp. It was a camp for Russian soldiers, but many Americans were in it. They were mostly dying of TB. Dog tags had been removed, so we couldn't tell which corpses were Americans and which were not.

The [American] company commander went into the town of Falkenau with a group of men. He stopped people on the street and asked them, "What about the camp? How do they treat them?" They said, "We don't know anything about the camp." He said, "Give 'em a shovel!" He grabbed a whole group of people—Germans—and marched them right into the camp. He made them take the dead, line them up row after row after row, dress them, put them in carts, lead the carts through the town, and then bury them.

I have all that on [16mm] film. Rough! Little things in there: They're throwing dirt down on a grave, and the face of a corpse is uncovered. These Hitler Jugend kids have to climb down, cover the face with a handkerchief, and then continue with the burial. Rough stuff! The dead are being carted through the town, and a little boy runs out with a toy rifle.

He doesn't know a funeral's going on. He goes bang-bang-bang-bang at the corpses with his rifle. I have it all on film.

Q: Did you feel that the people you met in postwar Germany were ideological?
A: There was no politics. Frustration, hunger, defeat, and wild kids, really wild kids: that's what it was like in Germany at the time.

Q: Why did you use Wagner and Beethoven so much on the soundtrack?
A: To me, Beethoven and Wagner—politically, spiritually, and musically—conflicted. That's why I was very wrought up with that. The rise of Hitler was told through Wagner. [*Fuller hums Wagner, progressively getting louder.*] That's the way Hitler did it. He started with one man, and then there were two [, then three, etc.] That's why I used the music a hell of a lot. And then it's great for the ending. Jesus Christ! Wagner and fire and blond boys and horses! Good God, how can you go wrong with that?

Q: The destructive forces in the film seemed to be running out of control.
A: Right. I tried especially to personify that in one scene, where the young German leader is told by another neo-Nazi, "We can't blow up these trucks because they're carrying medicine to the people. Now, we'll fight the damn Americans, and we'll lie and cheat and steal and kill. We'll do anything for you, but we need the medicine for the people." The leader says, "Oh, the hell with them." The other guy says, "But these are Germans!" And the leader says, "THE HELL WITH THEM!"

That's why, in *Verboten!*, I wanted to get the feeling of . . . you used the word chaos, which is good. I wanted to get the feeling of animal fury and viciousness.

The Crimson Kimono

A: One of the oldest expressions in sex is "Let's change our luck." That means, "Let's go and get a colored girl." I thought it would be a good effect if I reversed the whole thing, so that when the white girl falls in love with the Japanese fellow, he would say, "Now wait a minute. I want to make sure you really love me. I have a funny feeling that, just like whites 'change their luck' with a Negro, you're getting a kick finding out what it's like to get laid by an Oriental." I don't know why, but I left out those lines of dialogue. I don't know if [now] the idea comes across. One day, I'll hit it. At one time, I even planned on using that line of dialogue in

Run of the Arrow. I wanted to have the Indian girl think, "What is it like to lay a white man?"

But anyway, that idea got me started on *Kimono*.

There's a highly experimental flavor to that picture. The whole thing was shot downtown [LA] in Little Tokyo. Since I was shooting a lot of street stuff at night with hidden cameras, I had to use a very fast, sensitive film. I couldn't use any lighting. The opening scene was the most difficult I've ever had to do (and I've shot scenes with a thousand men in *Merrill's Marauders*). I hid three cameras, one on a roof, one in a truck, and another in a car. When the girl fell, at my gunshot, she fell in the middle of the street in traffic. We didn't stage it. That was real traffic. If some idiot had pulled out all of a sudden, the girl would have gotten it. Most dangerous scene I've ever shot.

Q: I like the contrasts in the ending. The killer is getting gunned down in the street, while all around are people in beautiful costumes with little jingling ornaments.
A: There's another place that I used music to establish contrast. Several bands are in that celebration at the end. One plays classical music, one plays Japanese music, one plays hot music, and so on. Whenever I cut from the killer to the pursuer, the music changed. That gave me the discordant and chaotic note I wanted.

I thought the end of the picture was very honest. I hate phony, lying losers. I hate scenes, and I've seen them a thousand times, where one fellow loses the girl to another guy, and the loser says, "Well, we'll still be friends. Don't worry." No! Not in my film. He didn't give a damn whether the guy was yellow or white. He was angry because the guy stole his girl. And he stayed angry.

Underworld U.S.A.

A: I figured I'd do [*The Count of*] *Monte Cristo*; I'd do Dumas. With one exception: instead of getting even with the guys personally, he [Cliff Robertson] uses the law to knock off the people he doesn't like. I thought that was a pretty good approach to the story.

Q: A theme of cleanliness runs through *Underworld U.S.A.* It starts with Tolly Devlin [Cliff Robertson] sterilizing instruments in a prison hospital and ends when, as he's dying, he stumbles over a trash can which says "Keep Your City Clean."

A: Again, I wanted contrast. In addition to sterilizing utensils, I told Robertson to put the bandages on the man very gently, very precisely, like a surgeon. I wanted to get that effect: he's clean about those bandages even though he's double-crossing the man he's putting them on.

I also tried to get a contrast wherever I could between the cleanliness of the head of National Projects and the discussion he's carrying on about narcotics and prostitution and murder. That's why I picked the swimming pool location. I wanted that hollow, clean atmosphere you get around a swimming pool. It's too bad we can't have smell in motion pictures, because there's an antiseptic smell around a pool, like in a gym. I thought that the cleanest thing in the world is a pool. So I had this crime organization hold their meetings there, rather than in the pompous office or the pool hall or the dingy little room where gangsters usually hang out. I wanted to get that contrast to what they're talking about: it's so vile and low.

Q: You depict National Projects, the front for *Underworld U.S.A.*, as such a typical business organization, with adding machines and bankers and everything.
A: It's all done mechanically, almost like robots, like computer systems. I don't doubt that crime today is governed by computers. If I were to make that picture today, I'd show nothing but twenty machines. No people, just all the machines. I wanted to get that flavor of mechanization in the picture.

Q: It seemed to be that crime was defined in *Underworld U.S.A.* as lack of emotion.
A: Yes. And also a facade of good citizenship. Remember that Boss Connors [Robert Emhardt] said, "All we have to do is pay a little taxes, go to church, send a couple of kids through school, set up a few charities on the side. We'll win. We always have. We always will."

Q: The coldness of the organization is particularly well reflected in [Gus,] the Richard Rust character, the paid killer. He commits his murders totally without commitment, almost casually.
A: Now there's an honest character! He's not a psychotic; there's nothing insane about him. He just has a job. He certainly isn't interested in killing that little kid. There's no vengeance in it. There's no emotion in the man at all. That's what finally terrorizes Robertson—the way Rust says, "We have to wipe out this girl. If you do a good job, it'll get you in

with the Boss." The only emotion he has is that it will get him in with the Boss. To knock off a girl means nothing.

I didn't want Rust to do anything that deviated from the character of a professional killer, except one thing. I told him, "When you're getting ready to kill somebody, put on your dark glasses. Then we'll never know whether or not you want to see anything, or whether or not you're feeling anything." You see, I wanted to keep away from emotion. I didn't want a character like in the old gangster pictures: he likes his mother, he supports his brother, he has a little dog, he feeds goldfish.

Q: Tolly Devlin [Robertson] is the only one in the film who acted on personal grounds. He wasn't motivated by a newspaper story; he actually witnessed his father's murder.
A: I used the same thing in *Pickup on South Street*. This is human nature: [Richard] Widmark didn't care about anything. Didn't care! But when he found out that someone took a beating for him, that someone was physically hurt who was tied up with him, he said, "O.K. That's it," and he went right after the enemy.

It's a theme I like in a picture. I never like a man to do something heroic for any chauvinistic or false premise other than emotional, personal necessity. If a newspaper says, "GREAT HERO SAVES 12,000 PEOPLE FROM BEING BOMBED IN A STADIUM," we know he didn't save 12,000 people. He saved *one*. That's what I'm trying to bring out.

Merrill's Marauders

Q: The theme of the fighter is carried over into your next picture, *Merrill's Marauders*. It's summed up when Merrill [Jeff Chandler] says, "As long as you can take another step, you can fight."
A: That's only 50 percent. I wanted to go beyond that. I wanted to show that when he says, "You do what I do," that means, "When I die, you die." That's the main thing I wanted to bring out. That's the Big Baby.

We shot the whole thing on location. When we were shooting in this little village in the Philippines, I noticed a little boy who kept following me. So I told Claude Akins, one of my actors, "I have an idea." This [scene was] improvised, and it turned out very nicely. The Marauders came into this town. They're resting; they're exhausted; they're hungry, but they're too tired to eat. The little boy came up and looked at Akins's beard. When he started to scratch the beard, that gave me another idea: feeding. So this old woman came over and offered rice to an American soldier—who, as you know, is the best-fed soldier in the world. When Akins [Sergeant Kolowicz] realized the idiocy and the stupidity, the irony and the shame, that he, a big, burly, well-fed man, was being fed by this scrawny old woman, he started to cry. That, to me, is more important than anything else in the picture.

Q: The film ended strangely, before it was resolved.
A: The ending was an abortion. I was originally going to end with a sequence of the airfield being taken. We were going to go out with a lot of action. They decided not to shoot it for two reasons, both of them money. So I said, "O.K. All we can do is end it where they're walking away and then fade out." Someone went ahead and put not only a narration there but also a stock shot of soldiers marching. Well, that was their business.

Shock Corridor

A: Originally, I don't know how many years ago, I wanted to do a film exposing conditions in the mental hospitals of the United States. Then I decided to do it as a fiction piece instead of a documentary exposé. I said, "The hell with it! I can pull a Nellie Bly!" Nellie Bly, you know, impersonated a nut for a while in the Wards Island insane asylum many years ago. So I thought I'd dramatize a fellow who goes into an asylum to crack a murder and winds up insane. I'm glad I didn't make it when I originally intended to. Even if it had been the same story, it wouldn't have had the same up-to-date flavor: the combination Oppenheimer-Einstein-Teller, the tremendous [James] Meredith situation, and the turncoats of Korea. So I put that all together, and I modernized it, and that was *Shock Corridor.*

I enjoyed making that picture. I liked the idea of using color before a man became lucid. When he's insane, and he's thinking of something, once we see color, we know that immediately after that he'll be rational for a few minutes. So each person had his own little [vision]. For the Southern soldier, I used Japan. When I went location hunting for *House of Bamboo,* I shot a hell of a lot of stuff with my own camera. That's what I used for his nightmare. I have about eight thousand feet of film on the Mato Grosso. I went there [in Brazil] once looking for locations, and I lived with the Karaja Indian tribe for six or seven weeks. I used that for the Negro's nightmare. In Peter Breck's nightmare at the end, the waterfall coming down is part of the Iguazu Falls in the Mato Grosso. I shot all of this in Cinemascope and 16mm. I didn't have it unsqueezed. All I did was blow it up to 35mm. So there it was, giving a weird effect without my doing anything.

Q: Was there any particular reason why Dr. Boden [Gene Barry] didn't have a visual nightmare but an aural one?
A: Oh, that was intentional. I don't know why, but I get a certain feeling when I think of a laboratory, Oppenheimer and all that. I see big buildings and big rooms—hollow chambers, little holes—and voices coming out. You know: "Dr. So-and-so, will you please report to so-and-so." I don't see phones. I see nothing but an intercom. A big, weird, almost science-fiction flavor—that's what I wanted to get. I also wanted one thing that sets Boden apart from the others: voices and, more importantly, the coldness of it.

Q: Of course, the great *tour de force* is the thunderstorm scene in the corridor. Could you discuss how you shot it?
A: Of course! I thought it would be fresh to show a thunderstorm just as if it happened right here in this room. I needed really a lot of water. Now, you must realize this was a dangerous situation, because there was no outlet for the water on this particular sound stage. You have to have a tank under the floor for the drainage. Otherwise, you can ruin a lot of equipment.

We didn't have any of these things, but I did it anyway, because I knew it was going to be the last day of shooting. I had to get what I wanted on the first take. To be very careful about it, I had a regular camera on [Peter] Breck and a second camera above that one, tipped down and shooting in close-up. I didn't want to have to stop; I couldn't afford the time. I had everything ready for me. The door was open, and my car was running. I had to make a hasty exit, since I'm chicken. I didn't want to be around when the studio manager came in and started asking a lot of questions. As Breck screamed, I waited twenty seconds. I wanted the biggest scream I could get. Then, I said, "Forget it!" and I ran out. I never went back—to the studio or the set.

Q: How do you evaluate the character of Dr. Cristo [John Matthews]? Do you find him sympathetic or noteworthy?
A: No. To me, Dr. Cristo is a symbol of all officials in a hospital. I dramatized him as being understanding *until* he becomes slightly suspicious.

Q: Cristo says, "You can't tamper with the mind," and implies that this is why the reporter went insane. But were you trying to say more than that: that everyone has this insanity inside of him?

A: Sure! I should have emphasized that even more strongly in the film. I should have made it clearer that for the reporter to want to do this, to volunteer to be accepted as an inmate, he had to be a little crazy in the first place.

Every one of us naturally has an inclination to yell or go crazy or break things. Even if you don't think that's a form of insanity, I do. I'm positive that, next to death, insanity is one of the most interesting subjects. I mean, I'm intrigued by it.

The Naked Kiss

Q: I think that *The Naked Kiss* is in many ways more "shocking" than *Shock Corridor*.

A: It is.

Q: In fact, I would say that it's the most shocking film you've made. It seemed that you deliberately went to lengths to get a reaction from the audience, especially when you pull the rug out from under everything in the child-molesting scene.

A: I wanted to bring something else out, but I don't know if I succeeded, because we were short on loot, the bastards. I had a scene where [Kelly] Constance Towers confronts the townspeople after they find out that she's innocent. At first they were ready to lynch her, and now they want vindication. She tells them to go to hell. I didn't shoot this scene—no money. She calls them hypocrites, which is all right. But the important thing is that she realizes how happy she was in her [prostitution] profession. She says, in effect, "What a thrill it is: when you get through laying any of those bastards, he pays you off and leaves. You don't have to listen to him or to his stories or to his lies, like I have to listen to your lies every day."

I thought it would be very effective if a girl kills a saint, and no one believes that the saint is really guilty of a horrible crime. That's the premise I wanted. How do I make this man saintly and canonize him? I made him the sweetest man in the world, with all sorts of charitable gadgets: hospitals, a town named after him, and so on.

So when I [conceived] the film as a shocker, the original impression I wanted was of a wonderful, almost dull, very, very ordinary love story: the poor girl from the wrong side of the tracks, the rich man who falls in love with her. Well, I hate those kinds of stories. So I knew I was going to have fun the minute she finds him molesting the child. Now, when you saw the picture, did that scene shock you?

Q: To say the least.

A: Good. That's what I wanted. I don't mean that I wanted it to shock you content-wise; I wanted it to shock you story-wise. A lot of people didn't like that picture. Certain friends of mine said, "Oh, why'd you have him try to lay a little girl?" I don't know, maybe they resented it because of some secret, hidden desire. What [did they] expect me to do? Suppose there's no child-molesting scene. I wouldn't have made the story. There is no story, as far as I'm concerned. I'm not interested in the girl from the wrong side of the tracks. They made those stories at Metro and Warners for fifty years: She goes to the right side, she meets the fellow, sometimes she finds out he's a nice guy, sometimes she finds out he's a phony, but there's always a happy ending.

Q: The opening scene is astonishing, where Towers beats up the pimp as her wig is falling off. The viewer is assaulted before the credits even come on.

A: Did that surprise you, that beginning? There's no fade-in, you know. We open with a direct cut. In that scene, the actors utilized the camera. They held the camera; it was strapped on them. For the first shot, the pimp has the camera strapped on his chest. I say to Towers, "Hit the camera!" She hits the camera, the lens. Then I reverse it. I put the camera on her, and she whacks the hell out of him. I thought it was effective. She had a difficult time making herself up at the end of the scene, because she had to use the lens as a mirror. As the titles come on, she's looking into the lens.

Q: There are many artistic references in the film, mostly connected with Grant [Michael Dante], the millionaire. The most outstanding ones are to Beethoven.

A: Ah! First of all, I wanted to show that the millionaire's a very "nice" man; he likes to sit and listen to music, and all that stuff. The girl is very hungry for something like that. Beethoven is a symbol. It could have been any other composer or artist.

Q: What were you intending with the imaginary trip to Venice during the big love scene?

A: I wanted that very badly for many reasons. First of all, I'm trying to sell him as a poetic, musical type—the fellow she wants so badly. She's never had anything like this before. The Venice scenes gave me a chance to show that pictorially.

But what I wanted more than anything else was to use that to build up to The Kiss, The Naked Kiss. I have him kiss her in the gondola, with the leaves falling. I cut on that position to them kissing on the couch. One more leaf falls. We'll never know whether that's in her mind or it really happened. The minute she kisses him, she draws away. He says, "What's the matter?" She says, "Nothing." That's when she should have said, "There's something wrong with you." But she didn't.

I had to have something highly molasses-like, even cornily romantic, in that scene. I couldn't just have them kissing on the couch. I had to have all that phony mood for one reason: I thought if I gave him an overload of gibble-gabble—about poets and painters and writers and musicians—we would understand why she doesn't object right then. I had to get a man who symbolized everything she was hungry for. I went overboard. I had to.

When she does find out this man's secret, and she realizes that he had given her a Naked Kiss, she's shocked, and he's shocked that she's shocked. Since she's a hooker, he thought that she would understand why he likes little girls.

Shark!

A: When I made *Shark!* I had what I felt was a brainstorm: doing a story about four amoral characters. One is a scientist [Barry Sullivan]: no morals. One is the girl [Silvia Pinal] he's laying: no morals. One is the young hero [Burt Reynolds]: no morals. One is the cop [Enrique Lucero]: no morals. I thought it would be interesting to show not only a double-cross on a double-cross, but when we think we know who the heavy is, we find out that the real heavy behind it all is the girl. She's the lowest. She does have a chance to get out of it alive, if she levels with the lead. But she doesn't. She is responsible for her own death. He lets her die. I tried something different there. They're in love and all that stuff, and I have the hero not only allow her to die, but he shrugs it off. I thought that was exciting.

I like the idea of a love affair where the man finds out the girl has used him. I gave her a great line of dialogue. The last line of the picture—now I find out that the producers have put it in ahead, and it's no longer the last line—she says to him, "We're both a couple of bastards—only I'm a rich one." That's the whole flavor I wanted. I shot some great stuff. For instance, when the boat is sinking at the end, he takes a lighted cigarette and throws it into the sea. I just stay on that cigarette. A fish sees it (the fish being a symbol of the shark), thinks it's something, and grabs it— pssshhht! [*Sound of a cigarette being extinguished.*] That's the end of the picture. Now I think they've cut it out. A lot of things like that were cut out.

As you know, I asked them to take my name off the damned thing, because I didn't like the cut I saw. I thought it was terrible. I told them I wanted to restore my original cut. They said they didn't know if they could get the film from Mexico. They couldn't locate it. It was such a confused state of affairs. Finally, I told them, "Don't bother me about it anymore." It may be the world's worst picture, or it may turn out to be a surprise to me. I don't know. I do know I had fun with the characters, because I went beyond the average switch of revealing the villain. I also didn't have a guy just letting a girl go off to jail; he lets her be eaten up by sharks. I've never seen anything like that in a picture before. Have you? That's my ending. That's what I shot.

The only reason I first called the picture *Caine* is that we went to a restaurant in Mexico where the service was bad. I got sore, and while I was getting sore, I felt like Cain, so I said, "Well, we'll call it *Caine*." That's all. Hell. I felt like hell. Then the producer saw a layout in *Life*, some pictures of a guy being killed by a shark or something like that, and it said, "Shark." So they changed the title!

Well, that's the checkered career of an ex-copyboy. That's thirty.

Samuel Fuller: A *Cinema* Interview

Ian Christie et al./1969

From *Cinema* (Cambridge, England), February 1970, 6–8. Reprinted by permission.

Samuel Fuller was interviewed at the Edinburgh Festival in August 1969 by Ian Christie, Nicholas Garnham, Angela Kirtland, Lynda Myles, Robert Mundy, Mike Wallington, David Will, and Peter Wollen.

Q: We'd like to start by asking you why you prefer camera movements to cutting.
A: To me it's a natural instinct. Let's say I want to shoot a scene with this group of us here. I don't think there is anything unusual or brilliant doing a pan shot from half-a-dozen different angles, and then let the cutting room put it together for me. I'd much rather bring in a camera and move it around. I'd plant somebody in here who is holding a gun under the table, and make it clear in the context of the movie that this guy has taken a religious oath to shoot somebody after fifteen minutes. I'd take the camera under the table to show the gun. . . .

Q: Hitchcock would give you a close-up of the gun. Why would you take the camera under the table?
A: I don't like head-on static shots. You know, what I don't like about movies in the last forty years is that the technicians have taken over. A cameraman will tell you how a scene should be shot. A director shouldn't think of the lights, the camera; he should be worried about nothing else except character, like a writer. But you have all kinds of problems from the studio. I mean, would a publisher tell a writer, "We want every chapter in your next book to be seventeen pages long"? Because that's what the studios do to me. So I like to produce my own pictures. Then I can replace whoever I want on the set.

I'm encountering a lot of these kinds of problems in trying to set up my next production, *The Rifle*, which will be a picture of my own novel. There's even a possibility that I'll shoot it in Korea if the loot is legitimate. If you're really interested in camera movements, let me tell you how I'm going to do a scene in *The Rifle*. I want a forty-minute take on the screen. A track of soldiers marching which will last for forty minutes. All the action will be on the move from fade-in to fade-out. This is a real experiment. There won't be any place for the action to stop for anybody. Normally, it would take three days' shooting to get something like that: forty minutes on the screen. With me it will take forty minutes. Now if you know about filmmaking, you'll know that a camera doesn't hold that much film. So I'm going to do what they do with projection machines in movie theatres: switch on the second projector before the first one is finished. I'll shoot this with four cameras. We roll the first camera and, after nine hundred feet, turn on camera two. The last hundred feet of camera one and the first hundred of camera two are identical. Then we hit from two to three, reload one. Then we hit from three to four, reload two. Then from four to one again.

I'll need to rehearse it for a week, but when it comes out I'll have real time on the screen—forty minutes as forty minutes. I've already written the script. There's an insane French nun—who'll be played by my wife [Christa Lang], because she [speaks] French and all that. There will also be a man who has swallowed his tongue. I'll have a legitimate physical disintegration of these people. And no one has to act. Everything is really tight and movement is difficult. I will tell the whole cast that if they stumble, don't delay because their fannies are being pursued. They'll have to keep on going to keep up with the cameras. Whether you'll like the picture or not when it is made, you'll have to admit that it's a *motion* picture.

Q: We'd like to ask you about your relations with your cameramen. Especially Stanley Cortez, who shot your last two pictures, *Shock Corridor* and *Naked Kiss*. They seem old-fashioned films, and they reminded us of Fritz Lang's *Secret Beyond the Door*, which Cortez also shot.
A: Well Stanley has been around for some time, and he did [*The Magnificent*] *Ambersons* for [Orson] Welles and also *Night of the Hunter* with [Robert] Mitchum. But you are quite right, my last two pictures are old-fashioned in many respects. Stanley and I talked about "hypo-ing" *Shock Corridor* to make it look a little more kaleidoscopic. Stanley would have liked it that way, but this was a low-budget picture. I told this to Stanley: "I love to see you working, Stanley, and making the kind of pictures

you like, especially as your brother is such a famous motion picture star, Ricardo Cortez. But, Stanley, we have to have a fairly academic-looking picture unless you want to go to the bank and draw out 600,000 bucks. Then we could have a very different type of picture." And Stanley said: "Oh no. That academic style suits me just fine." I love that man! Furthermore, Stanley appreciated exactly what I was trying to do on *Shock Corridor*. We were trying to show the corrosion of a man's mind. And I'd seen UFA pictures [from Germany] where they actually assault the camera. But I didn't want to do that and give the audience the impression that [the character] was twice as crazy as he was.

But you know I've worked with the best cameramen in the business. Hal Mohr is phenomenal, Jimmy Howe [James Wong Howe] is sensational. And Stanley is incredible. You know, when he photographed *Night of the Hunter*, he had a shot of Mitchum chasing the two children through a swamp. That entire scene was shot *interior*. Stanley had to contrive an illusion. To me that is a cameraman. You see, I know nothing about lighting. I hardly ever look through the finder—and with someone like Stanley Cortez, I don't need to. The only reason I ride the camera at all is because I move it around a lot, and I like to make sure the operator knows what he's doing. But I resent a cameraman telling me how to do a shot. Let's say I did it the way he suggests, it doesn't work, and the critics say, "That's the worst goddamned shot we ever saw." That cameraman isn't going to take out a full page in *Variety* to say: "That shot was my idea."

Q: Do your cameramen get alarmed because you move your camera so much?
A: No, but the camera operators do. I always seem to get a man who weighs at least three hundred pounds, with a big, big fanny—and you can be sure that when he swings around, one of those cheeks is going to knock over something on the set. I had a little picture called *The Crimson Kimono*—shot by Sam Leavitt, who did all the [Otto] Preminger pictures. I had to do a shot with the camera coming in from the street into a restaurant. The camera had to keep moving, but there was nowhere that the operator could go. We took out all the stalls, but the table there was stuck like granite, and there was nowhere for the operator to sit. I tried to sit him on the table and slide him along. But there was too much friction with his big fanny. So I said: "Get me vaseline." We dabbed vaseline on the goddamned table and slid him along. That operator was so uncomfortable. But we got the shot. I loved that operator, but I'll tell you one thing: he'll have to lose weight.

There is a similar story on another picture I made. It was a little, insignificant picture, but it was very important to me, and it was called *Park Row*. I wanted to shoot a sequence where I would alternate between interiors and exteriors, taking the camera in and out with me. I called over the operator, Al Williams, to ask him if he thought he could manage it. I said that once we've pulled back that grip, we're going to go as fast as possible. He said: "It's all right with me. You know, I used to shoot pictures way back." We did it, and he went flying fifteen feet. He really flew! I said: "Do you still want to tell me about those movies you shot way back?" It's so easy to shoot a sequence that alternates from the street to an interior in fifteen or twenty cuts. Another man might like to do it that way. But I hate that.

Q: Do you like being associated with violent pictures, or even with action pictures?
A: I don't care. I have a script that I was supposed to make in Spain called *The Eccentrics*. It had no action, and I'm crazy about it. It all depends on the story. I have a novel called *The Lusty Days* that has no violence. There's no violence in *The Baron of Arizona*, not too much in *I Shot Jesse James*, but *The Rifle* couldn't be done without a lot of violence.

Q: Your last three films have been like crusading journalism. You haven't compromised.
A: I'll tell you this: the man who was head of narcotics in Washington sent me a list of monies that the Department of Justice is cognizant of that are taken in every day in the USA for gambling, narcotics, whores, and labor bribery. I wanted to make a picture—with no plot—where at the end every mother and father would say to their sons: "Don't work hard. Don't go to college and get worried about a job with a pension. Go in to one of these rackets, for crying out loud, and make yourself 50,000 bucks a day." I thought this would be a new approach to making a movie. I shot a scene I was very proud of in *Underworld U.S.A.*, it was the best thing I ever shot, and it was cut out of the picture. It was the strike of the whores. The sit-down strike. It starts when a union organizer of the whores is killed in Chicago. I shot a big map of the United States. In Chicago, one girl crosses her legs. Suddenly Chesapeake, Bangor, Maine, San Diego, San Francisco, Denver, Detroit, and the whole map is filled with crossed legs. Then I cut to this big heavy who says: "Who started this goddamned strike?" It was out of the picture, and I was compromised.

Q: But in a sense your pictures are about compromise. *Run of the Arrow* shows us how society makes us compromise.

A: Somebody must have seen that, even if it was an usherette in Des Moines, Iowa. I wanted the [Rod] Steiger character in *Run of the Arrow* to be the basic root of all the hate that exists now in the South. That's why I liked *Easy Rider* so much. The man with the shotgun is today what Steiger was one hundred years ago. The people in the South are afraid of one thing in particular: not just that their way of life [might be] wrong, but that it will be forgotten. The Deep South has contributed absolutely nothing to American history.

Q: Did your background in journalism help you in films?

A: I think so. Everybody remembers something from their background. It's different if you live in a seminary. If you're a forty-eight-year-old virgin and this is a love scene, you're in a hell of a spot. My background in journalism helps me when I make pictures.

Q: Is that why *Park Row* is so good?

A: I remember the streets of New York during that time [the 1880s], and I wanted to recreate that in my picture. The cameraman [Jack Russell] said I needn't build the set to more than two stories, but I built it up to the fourth story and this is with my own loot—because I paid for that picture. The Studio would have paid more for it, if I had done it their way: with [Gregory] Peck, [Susan] Hayward, Mitzi Gaynor, and Dan Dailey—as a musical. But for me it was an experimental film, and I had to do it my way. They were all unknowns in *Park Row*: Gene Evans was just an extra who didn't even belong to the Actors' Guild. It was Mary Welch's first and last picture—she died. It was a very special movie for me, but it lost a lot of loot.

Q: Have you read Norman Mailer? I think you have a lot in common.

A: I don't know him, though I met him once. When *The Naked and the Dead* was about to be made at Warners, I was working there as a writer. He came into my office—a really nice guy. He said: "I understand you didn't like my book." I told him that I hadn't finished it, and that I didn't know the Pacific area at all. I didn't like some of his characters, especially the infantrymen. But that's neither here nor there. I told him: "You fought your War and I fought mine."

Q: Your War was in Europe, but most of your films are set in the Far East.
A: That's one hell of a contradiction. The Far East has always fascinated me. In fact, the only reason I made *Merrill's Marauders* was because I could make it in the Philippines, and I'd always wanted to go to Manila. The film was set in Burma, and I knew nothing about the Burma campaign, and nothing about General Frank Merrill [Jeff Chandler]. Most of the characters and incidents in *Merrill's Marauders* were things that happened to me in my War. Lemchek was my platoon sergeant. Also, I knew a guy called Kolowicz.

Q: How do you go about writing a script?
A: It depends on what kind of script it is; they're all different. I like to get a conflict, whereby a character is going one way and a situation is going the other way, and there is a clash. Like in *Underworld U.S.A.* where the law encourages [the gangster] Tolly Devlin [Cliff Robertson] to continue what he is doing. That's the kind of switch I like.

Q: We'd like to take the liberty of asking you about your politics. How do you vote?
A: I'm a Democrat, though not through any strong political preference. The only man who made the Democrats different from the Republicans was FDR—he brought back legal booze, and that was wonderful for the country. But he also introduced the doctrine of "the more you earn the more you pay" to our tax system, and that's very unfair to all our hardworking capitalists. They work very hard to make their millions of dollars. Most important of all, Roosevelt recognized Russia. That was one of the most important events of the twentieth century. But politics does not concern me in my pictures. If you write a story where the Red is a villain, you're a reactionary; if he isn't, you're a Commie. When I made *The Steel Helmet* one columnist said: "How does a Red get to make pictures in Hollywood?" But the *Daily Worker* said it was financed by General Douglas MacArthur. There are a lot of chicken-hearted liberals in the United States who make pictures, but never hit at anything. In *The Steel Helmet* I showed how the American government had a concentration camp in Arizona and they put the Japanese in it. That was never mentioned in the newspapers. But I'm not interested in who's a Red or an anti-Commie. If I feel that the hero should be a fascist, I'll make him a fascist. If he should be a leftist, then I'll make him one. I'm just interested in characters.

Proust's Madeleine, That's Pure Cinema

Dominique Rabourdin and Tristan Renaud/1974

From *Cinéma* (Paris) 193, December 1974, 84–90. Reprinted by permission of Dominique Rabourdin.

Q: Could you talk about shooting *Caine*?

A: When I got married to Christa Lang, who I met here in Paris, we went to Mexico for our honeymoon. That was a joke! I thought it was funny to bring my wife to Mexico on our wedding voyage, in order to make a movie there that I'd written in six, no five, days. Crazy! I told the Mexican producer I'd written it for children, the men living under the sea, and the sharks.

Q: After you finished the film, it was recut by the producers and retitled *Shark!*

A: I don't like [producers] making changes. Cutting things out. I have a lot of experience, so I'll say, "I'll make you a movie, and you can't change anything." [Producers] always say, "Of course not, never. " Yeah! I'm tired of fighting with rich people so they won't change anything.

Q: What about your film, which was going to be called *The Eccentrics*?

A: In 1968, I'm drinking at home, the phone rings, there's someone on the line who says, "I have money, I want you to work with me, I've already invested in *Chimes at Midnight*." I say: "You mean Orson Welles's *Falstaff*? Give me your phone number." I hang up. I call a journalist I know, who says, "This guy's for real." I pour myself another glass. I call the first guy, I say, "OK, some journalist told me that you're not a liar." He [Emiliano Piedra] says, "I'm coming to America with my associate." "What the hell?" I tell him. "You don't have to come to the United

States." He says, "I like to look people in the eyes." I laugh. It's like Gary Cooper, he wants to look me in the eyes! And they come, both of them. I tell them, "Write up the contract and give me the money." I get my bearings. I contact the actors, there was Jennifer Jones as the woman, Geraldine Chaplin as the girl, and Maurice Ronet—he was in France—as the man. I start building the set, a houseboat, a boat that you can live on. I need a special boat, otherwise I can't film. I need to raise the partitions, lower the floor so the camera can move.

Four days before filming, the youngest producer comes to tell me that an associate wants to buy his piece of the film and make it all himself. He adds: "I have just as much money as him. We're both going to court to say we're no longer in business together." I say, "I'm looking you in the eyes." I add the final word: "It's over, understand?" I didn't want to be making a film where there were relationships like that, associates bickering, wives set against their husbands, I don't like that stuff. Do people do that in the business world? To lose time, with all these personal problems?

Q: What is *Rialta*?
A: A film I made in Mexico two years ago. But the producer stopped the filming. They didn't like what I was doing. I think that I'm going to bring them to court because they owe me money. I'm thinking about it, I don't really like court cases. I've never fought a producer, but that guy went to idiot school, and graduated at the top of his class.

Q: Why did you write *Dead Pigeon on Beethoven Street* as a novel after the film?
A: When I finished shooting it, I went to Rome to do the editing. And this great German [literary] editor, who'd read the script in German, asked why I didn't make a book out of it. I told him, all right, and I wrote it in a hotel in six weeks. As for the film, I made it in Germany, but I made a really big mistake in using the crews there. It was a bad experience with the cameramen. Just terrible.

For the female lead, I didn't want one of those women straight out of the thirties or forties, a vamp. What a bunch of crap! I wanted a girl who looked like a spouse, a student, who is comfortable going into a store, who looks like everyone and no one, nobody extraordinary, who could talk to you and also talk to Willy Brandt. I auditioned some German women. Some femme fatales. Ridiculous! Then I thought of [my wife] Christa Lang, and I knew she could do it. That was the character I wanted. She said, "I'm not coming." She was going to a university, getting her degree. I told her, "I have to film in three days." And she told me that it was more important for her to earn her degree, and I told her that in fifty or one hundred years, movies will be different, but education won't be. And she came.

Q: How do you deal with what "really happened" when you write a screenplay?

A: When you tell a story, you have to lie and condense; otherwise the audience will drop you. I don't know if Proust lied at certain points, about the madeleine, for example. When [Swann] eats it, he sees his past, his mother, his aunt, the years gone by, that's for a great screenplay! It's visual. That's pure cinema. When you write a screenplay, you change things. Proust did that. He changed some of the things that his memory brought back to him. Because it was better that way. He put a character in here, and not there, because it was better.

I remember the part with [Swann's] mother, when she didn't say good night to him. He goes to bed, he waits, the door is open. He thinks that his mother is going to come and see him, she's coming, no, she's going somewhere else! That's great cinema. *In Search of Lost Time* [*Remembrance of Things Past*] needs to be on the big screen.

Q: Do you have other classic subjects for future films?

A: I have a script about Rimbaud, and another which is ready, about Balzac, I'll make it one day. I'm mostly interested in Balzac's human endeavors: you will never see him writing. Is that dumb? No, it's not; I just choose to forget that he wrote. The man, that's what counts. It'll be only at the end, once he's dead, that the word "writer" appears on the screen.

The screenplay starts with Balzac as a young man, just before he gets to Paris. I like him so much as a character, the son of a whore, the bastard, the snob, who kissed anyone's ass for a favor, a title. Jesus! He would have been in the middle of talking to you, and he'd see someone important, and say, "Just a minute," and run off to say, "How are you?" That has nothing to do with Balzac's works. It would be good for a movie, and I'll show it. That's all. That's how it is. At the end, I say, "The Académie [française] never recognized this man." Period.

Q: I'd like to ask you a difficult question.

A: Nothing is hard. Except death.

Q: In France, people say that you're anti-Communist.
A: I don't care. They're idiots. You know that that's idiocy, right?

Q: *China Gate* is dedicated to those who fought in the war against Communists. And *Pickup on South Street* is the same thing in a different context.
A: But why would I be an anti-Communist? If I made a movie about Lenin today, people would say that I'm a Communist! It's idiotic. I don't give a fuck about being a Communist, or a reactionary. You are never the same as your characters. If I make a film where some dogs are killed, that doesn't mean I like to kill. When I show combat, I'm not fighting. I make movies I like.

[My wife] Christa [Lang] is really radical. She's for the people, for the everyday men and women, and she gets really pissed off when people tell her that her husband is a fascist. If my movies or my characters get on my country's nerves, I'll make them anyway. I don't care. It's my characters that interest me. What we feel is what counts, and not the flags that we wave or the speeches we have to listen to. Knowing whether Stalin was right or wrong, whether Khrushchev was right or wrong, that's not important, that's politics. I'm not a politician.

When I made *Pickup on South Street*, I wanted to be honest about the people I was talking about, because I knew them. The informers, the girls who would sleep with anyone for a couple of bucks, the thieves, the pickpockets, I knew them, that's life in the United States. But they all think the Communists are beneath them. If you ask me what a Communist is, I don't know. For me, Russians are people, just people.

Q: Are there current politicians you have strong opinions about?
A: I can't like Nixon because he's a Republican, reactionary, and all that goes along with that. But I didn't like him instinctively, before he got involved with McCarthyism, I saw pictures of him way back, in California, I didn't know he was going to become Senator, but I didn't like his face. If I wanted someone to play the role of a really low guy, someone who smiles like a bandit in a western, I would use him. I don't like what he represents, and if he were here, I'd tell him what really happened with Watergate.

Q: You take an interest in your characters without trying to find out who is better, the executioner or the victim?
A: Unless it has to do with history, obviously. I love the history of the

United States, and I know it well, and I'm fully aware that about 90 percent of it is a lie, of course, that we're living the legend. [In France, also.] Think about the storming of the Bastille, a fascinating subject. I've seen reproductions of paintings made by a guy in 1790, in which the Bastille looks like the Empire State Building. [Here is] a more recent illustration, the start of legends. Young Mao and young Chiang Kai-shek were similar in the beginning. There were ten or twenty people, then one hundred, then a thousand, then a million, then in the end 750 million against Chiang. And he was defeated. That's history, that's a film I'd like to make. But if I make it, the reactionaries are going to say: he's a Communist. And that's stupid!

I have a story called *Generalissimo*. It's about a man who, at the end, is all alone on a boulder with people below applauding him, the conqueror. But he has to confront the truth: he's the conqueror of *nothing*. That, too, is history.

Sam Fuller's Suicide Note

Richard Thompson/1976

From *Movietone News* 50 (June 28, 1976): 1–8. Reprinted by permission of Richard Thompson.

Sam Fuller was twelve when, in the early 1920s, his father died and he moved with his mother and brothers to New York City from Worcester, Massachusetts. There, he continued his vocation: newsboy. "My mother did nothing—she was a mother," Fuller says. His brothers—one an excellent cartoonist—are now dead.

At fourteen and a half, he became Arthur Brisbane's private copyboy, going everywhere with Brisbane, then editor-in-chief of all Hearst papers. Fuller even rode to work in Brisbane's car, which was equipped with a dictaphone for each day's page-one editorial. At seventeen, Fuller wanted to be a police reporter. Brisbane said no; one had to be a good twenty. *The New York Graphic* called, looking for a head copyboy; Fuller demurred, saying he wanted to be reporter. *The Graphic* countered with an offer of higher wages and a quick rise to reporter.

The man who hired him away was Emile Gauvreau, who inspired both the play and the 1931 film, *Five Star Final*. As head copyboy, Fuller wrote every chance he got; he'd hand it in, and they'd throw it away, he recalls, "without interrupting the flow of the movement of their arms." Finally he was promoted to police reporter at $38.50 a week, $5 expenses. Per Fuller, *The Graphic* was full of crime and gossip.

This interview took place April 4, 1976, at Fuller's home above Laurel Canyon, where he lives with his wife, the actress Christa Lang Fuller, and their then sixteen-month-old daughter Samantha, Fuller's first child. Fuller works—and interviews—in the large converted garage of his home called The Shack, surrounded by about three hundred completed film scripts, all as yet unfilmed. (He adds six or so a year to the list.)

He still thinks of himself as a newspaperman, and he still speaks with the sound of New York.

SF: You can always tell about a leaper by the distance his toes are from the edge of either the window or the ledge of the roof he's threatening to jump from. If you're covering it, watch those toes. If they stick out, he's not a fraud, he's going, and he's going fast. He usually makes a silly speech.

[As a New York newspaperman,] I had collected a lot of suicide notes. When you cover a story, you ask the coroner, "Can I have the note?" Ironically, 90 percent of the notes end with: "God forgive me." No matter who the hell they are, they always say that before they're going to die. It's a fear complex. They turn to the only commodity sold to them and forced down their goddamned young throats: "God." It's silly.

I decided [in those days] I'd write a book called *God Forgive Me—God Forgive Me*, about all these characters, and reprint their notes. The best note I had was [from] this girl who wrote it with an eyebrow pencil on a small paper bag. "This is my Independence Day. Here is the way I am celebrating it. God forgive me."

I left the notes with my mother and went to Frisco. She was very panicky about them. My mother said, "How can you even hold on to these?" It depressed her. Every one of those little pieces of paper, by God, she lost them. It was just a terrible thing. It was my fault, I kept them all in a paper bag.

One of them was from three old maids, sisters, between seventy and eighty-five years old; they were panhandlers, beggars, they worked the subway entrances for money. Then they decided they had nothing to live for. They had eight or ten cents when a cop found them. They pooled their money and bought nightgowns and stuffed all the goddamned cracks and gassed themselves to death. This was my lead: "Three old, old maids joined the young in heaven yesterday." My night editor liked that very much.

Q: Your film *Park Row* (1952) is about the newspaper business in New York of the 1880s. You told me that, preparing the film, you became frustrated corresponding with the Mergenthaler Co. Their lawyers wrote back repeatedly trying to discourage you from dramatizing their namesake, Ottmar Mergenthaler, 1884 inventor of the Linotype.

SF: So finally I got a handwritten letter from Ottmar Mergenthaler's son.

He was then about seventy. He said, "This is just a matter of course, the lawyers [say 'no'] automatically." He wanted to subside my anger. I wrote him a letter telling him I didn't want anybody's permission, including his. Then he wrote me another letter saying, "Your anger interests me, you must think a lot of my father." So I wrote him, "I wouldn't have gone through all this unless I thought a lot of your father, and I'm going ahead with this project, and I don't want any further communication about it." I was pretty sore. So he wrote, "I'm inviting you to New York, come and see me."

Q: There's a still of you before a Linotype machine you used in *Park Row*. Where did you find the replica of Mergenthaler's invention? Or did you build it?
SF: I went to Mergenthaler Co., I met the son—wonderful man called Herman, he's dead now—he tipped me off to a man who had an old Lino machine here in L.A., and with a little mock-up, [this man] re-created the original blower, the forced-air machine that blew the matrix.

Q: So was Herman Mergenthaler now open to you including his father in *Park Row*?
SF: He explained that there's a certain funny feeling when people change characters around and, after all, it is his father. He said, "If I were to make a movie about *your* father, there might be little mannerisms that you wouldn't like, one weakness, one deceitful shrug, something." I could understand how he felt about it, even though his father was dead.

I said, "I can't, and won't, let anyone read the script, that's ridiculous. All I know is that I'm using [your father], and if I do anything wrong you can sue the hell out of me." He said, "I'll give you all the information you want." I said, "I don't want any information. I've known the character I want since I was a kid. I've read about him, I've heard about him, that's all I want." He said, "Fine."

Q: Did you have trouble casting the part?
SF: The actor, Bela Kovacs, looked just like Ottmar Mergenthaler, that's why I used him.

When the picture was shown for the American Newspaper Publishers' Association—that's an annual get-together of editors and publishers representing the dailies in this country—it was an unusual evening. The four Hearst sons were there with George Sokolsky, the very famous reactionary columnist for Hearst; and also, Douglas MacArthur, who was just fired by Truman and the next day was to go to Congress to make his famous "Old soldiers never die" speech. And former President Herbert Hoover. [*Fuller shows a still of himself with these luminaries at the event.*] I refused to let them release any publicity, including this picture—it's a great shot. Hoover, MacArthur, the four Hearst boys, and me. You understand, MacArthur was Page One, [the Republicans] were talking about running him for President.

Let's say MacArthur was a Democrat, let's say they were all liberals. [Even then,] I would have to say no. In my mind, newspapers are supposed to be above politics. They're not, of course. The thing is, we ran the movie, and naturally the newspapermen liked the picture, but that's not important. When it was over, Herman Mergenthaler grabbed me, hugged me, he was crying: he loved the way his father was portrayed. He gave me his bust of his father. Isn't that unbelievable?

In 1963 I went back down there [to ex–Park Row], and even *The World* was gone, with the big dome next to the Brooklyn Bridge. The only building remaining from when I started as a copyboy is *The New York Journal*. It's now a federal warehouse on Williams Street, right off the Bowery, around the corner from [what was] Park Row. When I was a kid and saw *The World*, I could use my imagination and think of [Joseph] Pulitzer walking in and out of those doors, and of the young [William Randolph] Hearst, three blocks away, taking over *The Journal*, and right beyond them were [Horace] Greeley and [James Gordon] Bennett, and [Charles] Dana of *The Sun*—Jeezus, it was a thrill knowing that once all these fellows were here. I always wanted to make a picture about [all] these men, but you couldn't. You'd need to have $25 million and do a biographical vignette of each running an hour, hour-and-a-half, a history of journalism.

[With *Park Row*,] I thought it'd be interesting just to make a composite. The thrill of that film was to have enough money that would allow for the reconstruction of that street. The only fictional addition to that whole damn set was the paper I created owned by the woman, Charity Hackett [Mary Welch]. Everything else was exactly the same.

My thrill also was having that streetcar. We really laid tracks, and really had cobblestones, and I even had the second and third floor built on the set. My cameraman [Jack Russell] said, "[The audience] won't see it, we're not going that high," and I said, "I don't care. As long as I can see it. I don't mind."

It was a UA release, and we opened in a [major] theatre I didn't want to open in. My ego said yes; in my heart, I knew it was the wrong house, because this was a very small black-and-white picture. It opened at Grauman's Chinese! I moved the Linotype into the forecourt, and when you bought your ticket you could have the man knock out your name on it. But *Park Row* died. Wherever it played, it died immediately. For me, it was a flop, though it didn't really lose money because it cost nothing. I shot it in fifteen days. It went on TV and did very well. It was revived, and did much better theatrically.

At 20th Century-Fox I had a chance to do [*Park Row*] under another title, and in color. Zanuck had a title called *In Old New York*. He said, "We'll make this into a big, big Technicolor picture with [Gregory] Peck, Susan Hayward, Dan Dailey." It was a fine cast; Dailey would be Steve Brodie and Mitzi Gaynor would be the barmaid, and there'd be a few musical numbers. Anyway, I turned it down. I'm not saying it's wrong or it's right, and I like Peck and Hayward, they're a class team, but it would have been a very expensive picture in those days. And I didn't like the movie title.

I was also approached by a man and wife music-and-lyrics team to do *Park Row* as a Broadway musical. You can do a musical about anything! Cain and Abel: [*sings*] "Would you druther / Kill your brother?"

Q: You broke Hollywood's rule and used your own money for *Park Row*?
SF: I sure did. Not all of it, but a lot of it. I don't regret that. If I had gone to UA or whoever who would have financed it, they would never have OK'd, for instance, that street set. They'd have OK'd only part of it. You're only supposed to build what you're going to shoot.

Q: What about the way the newspaperman, Phineas Mitchell [Gene Evans], operates in *Park Row*?
SF: He explains that, for competition, since he doesn't have a staff, he steals news, which they all do, they still do. He sends the fellow out for [*The Globe*], remember, and he tells him, "Use what you can and just change it enough . . ." and he didn't have to finish the sentence before the other man says, "I know what you mean." A lot of writers do that in books and in poems. As an editor, he doesn't feel that he's really plagiarizing. He is usurping and utilizing someone else's facts, but not [their] invention: that's the big difference in stealing from a newspaper. If you can't afford AP or UPI today, you just read them, and you say, "Oh my God, how am I going to rearrange this thing?"

What I'm trying to bring out is that every editor has his own approach, and his approach was—I hate like hell to use the word "honest"—it was a legitimate approach.

Q: But him telling that blowhard, Steve Brodie, to jump off the Brooklyn Bridge . . .
SF: Since in history [Brodie] kept telling everybody he was going to jump off the Bridge, I thought it would be funny for a guy to say, "OK, jump." And I knew in advance that it would be all right, because we all know he did jump off the Bridge and he lived to tell about it. That to me is a delineation of *that* kind of newspaperman, whereas Charles Dana of *The Sun* would not only discourage [Brodie] but would be a little reluctant about how in hell to handle the story. Because to him that was a vivid, exploitable, almost distasteful kind of copy. That's why the paper was shown as The Old Lady of Journalism, *The New York Sun*. [*The Globe*'s] the opposite, that's all.

Q: You frame your stories in terms of extremes, opposites: having the crusading editor beat the man's head to a pulp against the noble words carved on Franklin's statue.
SF: Well, I thought that was legitimate; the statue's there.

Q: But implicit is that the statue's there for beating heads on.
SF: That's the same as in a Western. The horses are there, and when there's a fight, you take advantage of the legs of the horses, you shoot through them. The best example in the world: when there was a firefight going on in the War, it struck me that many times we would fight in a graveyard, and the reason had nothing to do with dramatic contrasts or shock value, nothing. The run of stones there gave us excellent cover; we would instinctively, like animals, head to the stones, assuming bullets would not go through them. And then it dawned on all of us how ironic it was, that we were killing people where the people were already dead. We don't let them rest, we don't let them lie.

Q: I've noticed in your career how partial you are to musical numbers.
SF: Yeah? Well, I did have a song in *I Shot Jesse James* and I'll never do that again; a girl singing "Beautiful Dreamer"—it just kills me every time I think of it. I put it in because it was germane to that period, but I was wrong. Wrong because saloons at that time did not have entertainment of any kind. They had nothing but bums hanging around in the day-

time—most people worked. But if you walk into any saloon in a movie in the middle of the day, it's packed with people and there's a musical number!

Q: Why is *Park Row* so dark, with the characters materializing from shadows and disappearing into them?
SF: Illumination in those days was very, very dark; they didn't have electricity, they had gas or a lamp. They all had Rembrandt lighting, every one of them, just black, black with a certain grey. I wanted that. If it's bad photography, it's my fault. If it had been made at 20th Century-Fox, it would have been very, very bright, it would have been in color, the whole mood would have been different.

To answer your question: you just couldn't see too much in any of those offices. I told the cameraman, whatever your source of light, that's up to you, but—for instance, when a man walks into a set and lights a match, I don't want four lights to come up. We tried [my idea]: I darkened the stage, I lit a match. Well, he said, that's pretty weak. I said OK, use just a little stronger [light], but not much. And I thought it was an effective thing, to give a feeling that you have something that we take for granted, which is light. I don't know how many candles Balzac had [for writing], maybe two or three. Why in hell didn't everybody then go blind? During the War, we had Coleman lanterns. The slight touch of light inside gave us a warmth and a feeling of safety, that's because we could see each other. If you don't see each other, you feel each other, but it's much nicer to see. From a filmmaking point of view, pictorially, it's important to catch that feeling.

I had a very funny experience with Lucien Ballard, who photographed *Fixed Bayonets* for me. A scene took place in a cave. Well, I've been in caves and they're dark; that's why they're caves, especially if you get away from the entrance. "Here it is," I told him, "this is the scene, but no light." "Whattaya mean, no light?" "That's your headache," I said. "You're the professional." Just a joke! I walked away leaving a bit of egg on his face.

You are faking [illumination in darkness], and that can disturb an audience. I've seen scenes where someone says, "Kill the light!" and they do, and you still see [the actors] very plainly. You have to, because you have to see their reactions, but that to me is not good motion picture making. There instead, I don't mind depending on sound, whether it's heavy breathing, or a whisper, or the sound of feet shuffling: to me, that's much more dramatic.

Q: Did you see Bruce Surtees's dark, dark cinematography for *Play Misty for Me?*

SF: Oh, yes. The best photography I've seen in that vein was William Clothier in my picture [*Merrill's Marauders*]. I had just had an attack on the side of a mountain, and I set about thirty-six flags for explosions and it's about eleven at night, no moon, people were carrying lamps so they could talk to each other, one or two work lights for operating the equipment. Then I said, "All right, kill the lights. When I set off the explosions, that's when we'll see the men." And it worked beautifully. No lights, not one. You saw the men falling down and fighting and running and all that. And some of them you didn't even see, they were too far away, as the explosion wasn't powerful. That's the way it was. [Clothier] loved it. Any cameraman would.

I don't know anything technically about a camera, I really don't. The cameramen know. I tell them what I would like, and they give it. In *I Shot Jesse James*, the first time I ever directed, the first shot I did was the last in the ten-day picture. The last shot is where Ford [John Ireland], the assassin who had shot Jesse in the back, now is advancing on the back of the man who took his woman away, John Kelley [Preston Foster]. They said "day for night," and I didn't know what they meant. But I told Ernie Miller, who photographed it, I want it so black that there's only a little bit of moonlight coming. In Western towns, when the moon is at a certain [angle], it's all dark, and only between a couple of houses would a shaft of light hit the street. I didn't want it where the moon was high. I wanted black silhouettes all over. And [Ernie] did it and I liked it, but it wasn't perfect because he was still doing "day for night." He filtered it, it's not important, but I still think it's wrong.

You see on TV automobiles pulling up right past the camera and there's no shaft of light—they're shooting "day for night." When you have a real shaft of light, you'll see things in the air—dust, raindrops, things flying around—you'll see it in a room, including a hospital room. They're all filled with dust. When the light hits [a hospital room] in a certain way, ooh, it's horrible, for certain people; they'd have a hemorrhage, hypochondriacs would go crazy. That's what I miss in a night shot with a car. If there's no dust, it means it's a set.

Q: How do you organize your shots visually—the composition, the blocking, the camera moves, the editing?

SF: If I were writing a scene about you, and you shook your head and you smiled, I'd have to maneuver that camera in such a way—I don't want to cut—so that I can be on your eyes as they twinkle while you shake your head. The important thing, it's not the shaking the head, because if the camera's over there [in long shot] you can shake your head and we'll still see it, but we won't know whether you are laughing to yourself or whether you're planning to shoot me. You have to be in that close— the camera's very effective that way. So I judge it for the emotional reaction. I like shock cuts, and I love the idea of eliminating dissolves. I think they're very poetic, very nice, and highly boring to me unless there's an essential reason for a dissolve. [Time passing] was replaced [by filmmakers]—the dissolve replaced the intertitle, "The Next Morning." Then they went in for clocks, and sky and sun and moon and raindrops, snow, flowers, a dog, a full bowl, an empty bowl, all that nonsense. You don't really need that because, visually, you can go from one image to another within two or three seconds, even on a pullback. Establish that there is a lapse of time by what [a character] is saying, or by what he has done. For example: a man kills a man CUT TO a water faucet, he's wiping the blood off his hands CUT TO a car, he's leaving. Visually, it will progress. Tell a story with a camera the way you tell a story at home: "You know what this man did? He killed this fellow, and you know he just went in and washed his hands, and drove off in his car." That's exactly what you would say. Why not show it that way?

Q: No wonder you don't work for TV.
SF: The closest I've come to a car chase was in *Dead Pigeon on Beethoven Street*. I had one shot of a car chasing a car down along the Rhine. And the second shot is through a bower. That's all. I tried to cut that down, and I couldn't. I timed it, and it was four seconds."

Q: What's your objection to car chases?
SF: To me, there's no dramatic stuff involved, there's no inventive stuff involved, it's saturated. I don't like a car chasing a car unless something is different, something original.

"Being Wrong Is the Right Way of Living": An Interview with Samuel Fuller

Russell Merritt and Peter Lehman/1980

From *Wide Angle* 4, no.1 (1980): 66–75. Reprinted by permission of Russell Merritt and Peter Lehman.

Samuel Fuller, Hollywood director, was the guest of the 1980 Athens [Ohio] International Film Festival. He proved ideal for a festival dedicated to showcasing fiercely independent filmmakers. During an audience question-and-answer session, he explained that his films depart from classical narrative construction. Rather than situations developed leading up to climaxes, they are a series of shocks and explosions. Fuller himself is a never-ending series of explosions. Vigorous, enthusiastic, exciting, he delighted everyone he spoke to during his visit.

RM: The most common word applied to your films is "primitive." Do you like that?
SF: It doesn't bother me at all. In a way, it intrigues me. It gives me a picture of a hairy ape and a grabber of women's hair.

PL: What makes people call your work "primitive"?
SF: I don't know. It could be a very good compliment. If you say, "He was a wonderful primitive writer, or poet, or killer from Alaska," your mind runs from breast beaters to grizzly bears to Eskimos, according to the country.

PL: In cinema, most filmmakers look like they're working in the shadow of D. W. Griffith.
SF: That I like. That makes sense.

PL: But isn't your work unlike most work made after Griffith?

SF: I never looked at it that way. My original inspiration was John Ford's *The Informer*. For only one reason. Emotion! That film will give you every emotion you want.

PL: *The Informer*? You've talked about *The Ox-Bow Incident* in the same way. I found that puzzling, too. Both films are slow moving, the images classically composed. They're such pretentious movies, entirely unlike you.

SF: The treatment of the story, the telling of the story?

RM: Much different. Your work is a series of shocks.

PL: I greatly admire John Ford, but he works in Griffith's shadow.

SF: You're 100 percent right. He sets his camera. He does not make a moving picture. I'm excited about the camera being not just the eye, that's normal, but the actual mouth. It's the audience, it's going through a keyhole, getting under a bush.

RM: Judging from your films, you still believe in America as the best hope for refugees, orphans, the homeless. Yet the America you portray is a divided, racially disturbed, underworld with pimps, whores, delinquents, scum. Why would anyone want to be part of a country like that?

SF: Because a country like that, no matter how disturbed, confused, or low, is a ship with a deck. It has been proven far more inviting than other decks all over the world. Now America might have twelve Captain Blighs, and they might flog the hell out of you even before breakfast, and blood runs down the goddamn deck, and the real skipper of the ship is hypocrisy. But it's not sinking.

RM: America is the best we can expect?

SF: No, America is about the worst we can expect. [Even if it's] the best of all existing nations. Very terrible. But it's young. It's a baby, don't forget. It's wet and we are wiping its ass. I don't know why everyone like you says, "You show the pimps and whores." We *have* that in the United States—pimps, procurers, Nixon. There's nothing wrong in that, my God.

RM: But there is something wrong in that.

SF: It's wrong when they're caught. Aha!

RM: It's wrong when they do it.
SF: This has been going on for ten thousand years.

RM: That doesn't make it wrong?
SF: Being wrong is the right way of living. We have been brought up like that since 10,000 BC. It started with a man and a club. The club developed into a sword. That's the birth of royalty. That's the birth of power. Take a look at any goddamn nation. How do you think it survives?

PL: I'm struck by the specifically American dedications that you gave to several of your films—the American press, the American military. The Army.
SF: No. No. Not the Army. Oooh, I'm very touchy about that. I dedicated [a film] to the US Infantry. Now the Infantry is a very special thing to me because they are actually said to be expendable. I could have said, "Dedicated to 7,800 number 745s," but to the audience that wouldn't mean anything. In an Army death list, a 745 is a rifleman. When you die, it's a rifleman; it's not you; it's not a name. I see lists, lists, lists, of how many 745s have died. We have progressed to a point where when men die, they have become numbers. See, a rifleman is the lowest form in the Army. That's a very personal thing to me.

RM: Is that what your script for *The Rifle* is about?
SF: *The Rifle* is about Vietnam. If I have enough money, then I'll show you a Vietnam story, for Christ's sake. These other Vietnamese stories are shit! In my story, it's the American point of view, and the Americans are right. CUT. We go to the VC point of view, they're right. CUT. Chinese point of view. CUT. Russian point of view. Every point of view. We put them all together at the end. They're not only full of shit, they're the biggest hypocrites in the world.

PL: That would be different from *The Steel Helmet* or *China Gate*, where only the American point of view, or the Western point of view, is expressed.
SF: That's your story! I didn't want to go into "guilty" for *China Gate*. I was interested in a half-dozen men from different countries. Everyone is using [Indo-China] as a battlefield.

RM: But that's not your perspective in this film. It's not that Indo-China is being raped by assorted countries. In your prologue, you make it very

clear that your sympathies are with the French cause. *China Gate* is a paean to the French forces liberating Indo-China from the Communists.
SF: I don't think I headed that way. I bring out a French viewpoint?

PL: It's the voice-over which gives authority to that perspective.
SF: What does the narrator say?

PL: That Russia is causing the turmoil, and that the French are the last to stand up to them.
SF: OK, I got it. You are saying that the finale of the narration brings it down to only one viewpoint. That one country, Russia, is coming in and another country, France, has to kick this country out.

RM: That's right.
SF: I see what you mean. That does not bother me at all, because it was true. Russia did not give a damn about Vietnam. They didn't call it colonialism, but that's what it was. That's the hypocrisy of it. They are phonies, we are phonies, but we are honest phonies. We want the buck, they say they don't want the buck. They want "kopeks," but they won't come out and say it. That makes me laugh!

RM: Of all your films, what is the one you most want your daughter to see?
SF: I don't know. She's seen several of my films. She saw *The Big Red One.* I was not with her. She's five. And when she came back, she said, "Why did Daddy have a man shoot flowers?" And I said, "Well, he was not hurting the flowers. He was shooting past the flowers to kill someone." She loves flowers. She loves insects. So I tried one more time. "Remember when you went to camp? This is a camp where they kill people. I want you always to remember this—that all the time while they're killing people, the people who kill people are growing flowers. And they water them just like you do, and they're beautiful." But then I stopped because she couldn't grasp it.

You see, in this scene there's the death house and the ovens. And do you know what it was really like? I never saw this in the movies. The guards grew flowers. They had fun, and . . .

RM: In the concentration camp?
SF: Of course. Every time I see a concentration camp in films, it's always bleak. It's kind of gray, the big gates open. No, the camps we saw were

relaxed. The guards lived there. You know how a prisoner will grow a garden? Well, a guard will grow a garden, too.

RM: Similarly, the pervert in *The Naked Kiss* loves beautiful things. A little child he molests brings him flowers. He loves Beethoven. In fact, it is frequently the case that those characters who share your preferences for high culture are perverts, are wrong in some psychological way. What's behind that?

SF: Well, I'll tell you, Grant [Michael Dante] was a symbol—in this case, of America, specifically the Midwest, [of respectability in] a nice little town like [your] Athens. A lie was in the air. It was created by people who were Grants—the character's [family]. They belonged to organizations, a line of DARs or Kiwanis Club members. Whereas, the hooker [Constance Towers] is a symbol of someone who cannot even get into [their] neighborhood.

Now [about] the two hard-working people: his hard work may be in charity. Deciding if the needy people really are needy. Her job is laying. Of the two, I prefer her. [His being a] pervert is a symbol, too. Of course, all hypocrites do not go around molesting children. But for a motion picture to get an emotional impact with the damn people, I say hit it and hit it hard. I don't go to a lectern with [Bishop] Fulton Sheen behind me and talk for five hours. I saw this as a very good story to show what happens when a person from one civilization goes into another.

PL: Are you saying that high culture—classical music, Beethoven—would be part of that kind of . . . ?

SF: I put that in for one reason—that's story writing. She now has a hook with the man, and [it's] Beethoven. It doesn't have to be that. It could be art. It could be a piece of furniture. She might come in and dream—one day she would love to buy an authentic Queen Anne's chair, and she walks into [his] house and there it is. It's the thing that makes her mind explode. So she falls for him. Now he represents everything she has a hunger for, [and] she knows she has the intelligence to appreciate and accept these things.

Along comes this horrible curtain, her whole world (it's not just artistic but a sensitive world) collapses. [However,] she found peace within the confines of her own mind, [and with] the privacy of her own appreciation of art and music. She found more respect, and above all—that's my story—more honesty.

Now a lot of people don't like the picture. People didn't like the idea of [showing] what we call a nice middle-class community and exposing it. I'm not just exposing this community. I'm exposing the fact that we are unadulterated and highly dedicated bullshit artists.

PL: At the beginning of *Shock Corridor*, you quote Euripides. Beethoven comes in for *Dead Pigeon on Beethoven Street*. The characters in the films are not the kind who would be interested in such things. What does that mean to you?

SF: To me, it's humorous. I like you very much for bringing out one little thing I enjoy. It doesn't have to be [a Beethoven] museum. It could be anything. [In] *Dead Pigeon*, the American private eye could have been told] that a barge just sunk with forty-two thousand kids, or these are the spectacles that Beethoven wore, or the ear trumpet [Beethoven] wore. [All] he wants to know is, "What do I do now about the money?" In *Dead Pigeon*, the Beethoven house is important to me because I was in it one night during the War. I decided it would be wonderful to use it.

PL: Many characters in your films talk about how their parents taught them hatred and bigotry. Do you feel you were brought up to have narrow views?

SF: On the contrary. My mother was the most broad-minded woman I met. [Two ways she was narrow-minded:] she couldn't believe homosexuals exist. She couldn't believe that hookers have pimps who live off them. I said, "You must have known that when you were a girl." And she said, "I didn't . . . there can't be anybody like that."

RM: You never mention your father.

SF: Oh, he died when I was between ten and eleven. I didn't know him well.

RM: Were you a good student?

SF: I was kicked out of high school.

RM: How did that happen?

SF: Well, the night editor of *The New York Graphic* said, "You are going to George Washington High School?" This was the biggest high school in New York, and the first coed one. He said, "There are some teachers there hanky-pankying around." Which I didn't know about. I didn't care. "You're going to that school. We'll send a photographer." Unbeknownst to me, the [news] desk didn't like the Superintendent of the New York

Board of Education. A personal thing. So they picked this idiot, that's me. I was supposed to bring a [photographer] up to this recreation room, where the teachers got together to bullshit. He [hid] in a terrible position, behind the couch. What he wanted was a sex bullshit thing.

The photographer took pictures, and there was a flash. He scared them. But nothing was happening. A couple might have kissed, and they were telling dirty stories. There was no sex, actually. [But] I enjoyed it because I felt there was melodrama going on here. We were hiding, hiding, and this was evil, wrong, it was spying.

The paper came out. Page One. I was called to the auditorium. The principal was on stage and crucified me á la Judas Iscariot. He said, "If there is anything wrong going on at this school, you should have come to me. We're only interested in cleanliness and godliness." And he said, "Whatever you own, you take now. And anything owned by George Washington High School, any book, anything, you leave." He made me very happy [expelling me], because that meant a day job [in] newspapers.

RM: Would you like to make a film about an artist?
SF: I have my story. Did my research. It's called *Balzac*.

The tape stops here, but Samuel Fuller continues, caught up in his *Balzac* script. It's a tribute to a lifelong idol whose novels he has read since adolescence. It's also a reproach to the Académie Française, which has yet to admit Balzac to membership.

Rough Trade on Ivar Boulevard: Griffith Meets Sam Fuller

Russell Merritt/1980

From *The Griffith Project, Volume 12: Essays on D. W. Griffith*, edited by Paolo Cherchi Usai (London: British Film Institute, 2008). Reprinted by permission of Russell Merritt.

This is best told, I suppose, as a long-ago bedtime story about D. W. Griffith. It could also be called, "How I Bonded with Sam Fuller (Sort of)." But it's really an account of how Griffith appeared in the wild-eyed vision of one of America's great maverick directors, and how Fuller gave the father of film a new kind of patrimony.

My conversation with Fuller took place, appropriately enough for him, in a noisy downtown Ohio bar. Fuller, the guest of honor at the 1980 Athens International Film Festival, was holding court off-hours at a large table amidst smoke and low-slung lights. I joined the party, and learned he already knew I was working on Griffith. He asked me a few questions ("What's your angle? What's your hook?"), and then turned away. Later, as the conversation with the others grew stale, he turned back to me.

"You know what's wrong with you?" he said. "You're too old, and you lack imagination."

Unimaginative? Too old?

I was a little more than half Fuller's age at the time, but otherwise the elder at a table of college kids and hangers-on. Fuller had been pushing the crowd to make movies. Mainly he was listening to story ideas, and making connections to his own work. I was the sorrowful example of what happens when you choose, instead, an academic career.

He continued, with me as target.

"If I could do it, I'd put a sharpshooter on the roof across the street, and when you came out, I'd have him shoot you between the eyes! You're sitting on a great idea and you're too dumb to know it."

How long was I supposed to be polite? But maybe this requires a bit more context which, the reader needs to be warned, will only grow relevant as the story unfolds. In describing my Griffith angle, my hook, I had mentioned an enormous photo collage from Griffith movies that Griffith's adoring grandniece, Geraldine, had constructed on the occasion of his sixty-fifth birthday. Fuller had seen Griffith in a book posing with the collage, and wanted to know what happened to it. I told him. For this I was going to be killed?

Not exactly. But, then, he was just warming up.

"Listen to me!" He held up his hands, as if he were framing a shot, holding his cigar erect. "You start on the ass of a whore."

I had no idea of what he was talking about. But he had my undivided attention.

"Keep the camera tight on her ass. I want it in black-and-white. Grainy. It's night. Make the music greasy. Then, get that ass moving. Make her GRIND those cheeks! And—KEEP UP WITH HER!!"

Keep up with the ass of a whore?

For Fuller, it was all to be in one shot. The camera was to follow her to the street corner; stop when she left the sidewalk, tilt up slightly to see the street sign—Ivar & Hollywood—and then come back down to find her across the street, talking to two johns.

He continued.

We get close enough to hear them talking. They go back and forth. She wants twenty dollars; they'll give her ten dollars, maybe more if she shows them some nice tricks. They walk to the cheap hotel behind them. The camera—"DON'T CUT!! Just stay with them!!"—follows them up through the small lobby, up an elevator—"Make one of the guys short and bald, and have him knee her when they're close in the elevator, just to keep it interesting"—and they get out. The two men have the girl knock on a door. The door opens. A bewildered old man looks out. The johns shove the girl aside, rush inside the room, and throw the old man back onto a chair.

"The camera cuts to a tight close-up on the old guy. Voice over: 'WHEN I FIRST MET D. W. GRIFFITH, HE WAS DRUNK!'

"CUT!!! CREDITS!!!!"

What was this all about? Fuller was remembering Ezra Goodman's notorious interview with Griffith published in *PM Magazine* in 1948, in which Goodman and Seymour Stern used a secretary to gain access to

Griffith's hotel room. In the Fuller version, the interview was to provide the frame story for a low-budget action picture which, if he were to let me live, I was to write. The secretary was turned into a hooker!

Fuller knew nothing about the real-life Goodman or Stern, and had no interest in them. "Your hook," he told me, "is the whore. Make sure she's got blood on her mouth from when the guys shove her out of the way. Have her knock her mouth on something when she falls down."

The point was to give her something to do while a befuddled Griffith gradually agrees to answer Goodman's questions about his movies. She's bored and quiet, but she wants her twenty dollars. She's pressing a cold towel to her mouth; she's wandering around the room, half-interested in an enormous collage of photos from Griffith's films—Geraldine's collage—now mounted on the hotel wall.

The whore would stare at the stills. She would also find Griffith's straw hat on a coat rack—similar to the one Griffith wore while directing *The Birth of a Nation*. Fuller needed this to connect to Griffith at work in 1914—Griffith sitting inside a tent having his head shaved bald amidst the chaos of preparing for *Birth*'s battle scene. Cameraman Billy Bitzer, assistant directors, secretaries, money guys are all coming in and out, giving Griffith things to sign, calling for him, looking for direction. At the end of the scene, the barber would hold up a mirror, A bald-headed Griffith would stand, put on his straw hat (the one Lillian Gish describes with the large hole in it to let the sun rays through) and then walk out to direct his scene. Fuller said we could come back later to the battle scene itself. If there was no money to pay for it, we could cheat and not film it.

Fuller wouldn't leave it alone. On another occasion at Athens, Fuller returned the conversation to Griffith and "our" movie.

His idea was to have the prostitute steal the hat and, at the end of the film, walk off with it—and her twenty dollars. Then, sudden inspiration from Fuller—"This is a piss cutter!!"—she is to wander down into the lobby, and find the bar. At the far end, a man—"an African American, a colored guy"—is playing piano. Cross-cut to Griffith and his interviewers back at the room while the whore flirts downstairs with the piano man. Back and forth until we're finally at the bar where she's dancing and playing with the hat and the black guy. Then, just before she leaves, she tosses Griffith's hat on the piano man's head. And sashays out. "Use it!!! It's a goddamn, mother-fucking piss cutter!!"

Griffith meant a lot to Fuller. Although he called John Ford his "original inspiration" and *The Informer* his favorite film of all time, Griffith movies, he said, gave him energy. He recalled how he took the bait when

Darryl Zanuck jokingly challenged him to write an unfilmable script about the movies. Fuller's idea: start with a scene of the Ku Klux Klan riding to the rescue in *The Birth of a Nation*. The camera pulls back to reveal that the movie is being projected on the side of a barn. We see the 16mm projector on a table; the projectionist; and men in overalls watching it. One guy passes a pouch of chewing tobacco. We're at a Klan recruiting rally, and the gist of the dialog is that this is the best goddamn movie ever made.

Fuller had another way of connecting Griffith's life to his art. We said goodbye at the local airport while he waited for his plane and I waited for mine. We ended where we started: Fuller coming out of nowhere with a surprise punch. Up to this point, our airport conversation had been desultory, but Griffith, as ever, had become our *lingua franca*. Without warning, Fuller rapped me on the arm. He had one final bit of advice. I was to be "goddamn sure" that I got into the script what made Griffith a brilliant filmmaker. The secret wasn't the technical innovation. It was that Griffith lived all his life in a dream world—of feeling, sensation, and emotion—and found the power to transform it into a tangible universe. It's the kind of gift, Fuller said, that leaves you defenseless in the real world. "When you write about Griffith, you gotta remember that."

Cigars and Cinema with Sam Fuller

Gerald Peary/1980

From *The Real Paper* (Cambridge, Massachusetts), May 4, 1980. Reprinted by permission of Gerald Peary.

He resides way up in Laurel Canyon, in a narrow, outdated, unglamorous house that Phillip Marlowe could have inhabited in the 1940s. At this very moment you can be sure that Sam Fuller is puffing a long cigar, pounding out yet another script on a ratty typewriter, or reminiscing with a visitor—usually someone less than half Fuller's sixty-seven years—about his golden days as king of the "B" directors, even though he insists he makes "A" pictures on "B" budgets. In France, Samuel Fuller is practically a national hero, adored by a generation of cineastes led by Godard and Truffaut and Claude Chabrol. In America, only the most dedicated film freaks catch Fuller's twenty pictures—usually in black-and-white and tough all over—on the late, late show. Know these titles and you've got a grip on some of the best of Fuller: *The Steel Helmet* (1950), *Pickup on South Street* (1953), *Forty Guns* (1957), *Underworld U.S.A.* (1960), *Shock Corridor* (1963), *The Naked Kiss* (1965).

These are championship movies, though Fuller's career seemed permanently TKO'd in 1967. He was taken off *Shark!*, with Burt Reynolds, and wasn't that the end of it? For the next decade, Fuller sat home, dreaming movies. And befriending every fledgling screenwriter to hit Los Angeles. He critiqued their work for free, for love of the cinema. Finally, Peter Bogdanovich, a Fuller maniac, helped get financial backing for Fuller to write and direct a film based on his World War II army experiences in Normandy and Italy, a project that has obsessed Fuller for more than thirty years. That film, *The Big Red One*, is finally in release. I'd come to L.A. to converse with Fuller about it.

I had been warned: Sam Fuller talks your ear off, and *The Big Red One*'s existence has much to do with Fuller's almost unbelievable motor-mouth perseverance. In a studio meeting, he recited the plot in such enthusiastic, infinitesimal detail that Lorimar Productions practically agreed to do the film to quiet him. "Can't anybody shut this guy up?" is a famous quote from an exhausted Lorimar executive. Film critic Joseph McBride sat with Fuller and a tape recorder, planning an interview book on the question-answer model of *Hitchcock/Truffaut*. McBride gave up, overwhelmed. As he told me, "We had eighteen hours of tape and we'd only gotten to 1928." About six years ago, my pal McBride asked Fuller to play script doctor for a treatment of our mutual concoction—a John Fordish nostalgia Western. Fuller went through it, cut it to size, told McBride what the plot should be, and gave us a punchy title. All for gratis. When I met with Fuller, he looked worried only once: he just couldn't quite remember our very unmemorable almost-script.

I must brag: I received one of the shortest audiences with Sam Fuller on record, only three hours of straight talk. I succeeded in part by forcing questions into Fuller's non-stop happy-hour monologues. But mostly it was because Fuller had to pack his suitcase and leave for Cannes that evening; and he did apologize, again and again, for eventually kicking me out. He gave me presents of two of his novels, and autographed them.

Fuller was such a nice guy: buoyant, speedy, lovably crazy, prancing up and down his home office—"The Shack"—a dusty Salvation Army store of out-of-print books, endless Fuller scripts, scraps of memorabilia, and rancid cigar air from decades of non-stop puffing. Fuller stalked his study, acting out a scenario he was making up on the spot, about Nixon and Watergate. "Gerry," he said, slapping me on the leg, "I can see it!" His eyes twinkled deliriously, "Tricky Dick walks into the room!" Fuller played several juicy Washingtonians, including a rasping Kissinger. "What a picture it would make!"

Fuller thinks pictures. A few moments later he was whacking me on the thigh and bouncing another wild idea. He had me starring in a spy melodrama in his head. "We have a car! We have a shack! We have Peary! We have a man in a phone booth!" All exclamation points! All light bulbs! When I mentioned his birthplace, Worcester, Massachusetts, Fuller shouted "Woostah!" with proper accent, but he hadn't been there for years. He hadn't read my Cambridge, Massachusetts publication, *The Real Paper*, either, although the ex-tabloid scribe exclaimed, "I heard I'd love the sheet!"

I shifted him to war movies, the Fuller forté, because *The Big Red One* is only one in a long line of Fuller-directed military yarns, including *The Steel Helmet*, *Fixed Bayonets*, *Hell and High Water*, *China Gate*, and *Merrill's*

Marauders. There's the charge by critics that some of these are xenophobic, anti-Communist films.

"That's stupid," Fuller snorted. "They assume that you are in sympathy with your characters, but I don't care if my characters are American, Russian, or Nazi. If I made a movie about William the Conqueror, now nobody would give a damn. But in 1068, the people right away would have said, 'Why are you favoring this dictator?'"

Fuller, a lifelong Democrat, hates Nixon, but could see making a movie about him. He'd like to do one about Joe McCarthy. With mention of the late Wisconsin senator, Fuller again boiled over with celluloid excitement. "McCarthy goes into his apartment. The girl says: 'How's it coming?' He says, 'If I can put the screws to these bastards, I'm on the cover of *Life*. These are fucking schmucks.'" Fuller's cigar puffed like a steamboat picking up speed. "Gerry, I would take it from his point of view. I would love to tear the heart of an audience with the lousiest son-of-a-bitch ever going. Why don't they make this movie?"

We shifted subjects, to Sam Fuller's acting career, his colorful bit parts in Godard's *Pierrot le Fou*, Dennis Hopper's *The Last Movie*, Wim Wender's *The American Friend*, Steven Spielberg's *1941*, and the one role that got away, Meyer Lansky in *The Godfather Part II*.

"I'm crazy about Coppola. He tested me for the old Jewish gangster, and I did it with Al Pacino. But they thought I wasn't old enough or sick enough." Fuller promised me his *Godfather* screen test the next time I'm in L.A. He has the footage. But wasn't he sorry that this plum went to Lee Strasberg? "Naw," Fuller shrugged, a man without bitterness in his still-wiry body. "That man was perfect. And I'm very fond of Coppola's picture, *Apocalypse Now*, and its screenwriter, John Milius."

A few minutes later, as if planned, director John (*Dillinger, The Wind and the Lion*) Milius rang up. The guy who wrote the great Robert Duvall battle sequences in *Apocalypse Now* had just seen *The Big Red One*, and loved it. Fuller put me on the phone, and Milius delivered a stream of *Big Red One* blurbs to take back to Cambridge and *The Real Paper*. "It's wonderful, wonderful. I'm deeply jealous. I only wish I had made it." Fuller beamed at this heartfelt testimony from the New Hollywood for the best of the Old.

Samuel Fuller: Survivor

Tom Ryan/1980

From *Cinema Papers* 30, Melbourne, Australia (December–January 1980–81), 423–26, 498–500. Reprinted by permission of Tom Ryan.

Q: You seem to have heroes and heroines in films like *China Gate* and *The Naked Kiss* who live on the borderline, or outside of middle-class morality, outside the law.
A: I think they make the best characters, anyone who is involved in what we call "the lower depths," whether it is Dostoyevsky with *The Idiot*, Jean Valjean in *Les Miserables*, the Count of Monte Cristo, or anyone who has been double-crossed by society. The melodramatic characters seem to last, and they ensure much more interest, as far as the reader or viewer is concerned, than the saintly do-gooder.

Q: Are you deliberately confronting your audience by making them empathize with these outsider characters?
A: No, I'm only concerned that these people, whom I call "Gutter People," have their own code of honor. Even though I might not agree with them, they have a code that interests me. I met quite a few when I was a reporter. I found out that their way of thinking and living, ironically enough, had more solidity than the saintly people. They were thieves, pimps, and whores, very low people. But they stuck together in a way that the churches would like to have their congregations unite, though they never do. The "Gutter People" don't try to live on lies—but we do.

I would rather tell the story of a whore than a sweet girl who comes to the city and meets a young good-looking man, marries him and raises children. I don't see anything dramatic about that. It might be dramatic to other writers, but I couldn't write that kind of copy [or screenplay].

Q: One finds oneself within asylums in films like *Shock Corridor* and *The Big Red One*. The madness is linked to those characters who are the outsiders, who had been on the periphery of society.

A: As far as I am concerned, we are one big asylum, though we shake our heads and say, "Tisk, tisk, tisk" when we see outsiders who are abnormal or mentally sick. I've covered some insane asylums in my day, and the true story I wanted to tell, I couldn't tell. At the beginning of *Shock Corridor*, for example, I wanted to show, as the journalist passes them entering the asylum, naked men and women chained together on benches in a long corridor, sitting in their own filth. The Hollywood censor board refused me permission. I produced photographs from several mental institutions showing this was no fabrication, and they still said no. So I said, "The hell with it."

I wanted to do a story of the maltreatment of patients, the insane people, by sane people who really are acting insane, who have nothing but contempt for anyone who is "sick." When a man breaks a leg, or has a physical sickness, we say, "Too bad," and we don't shy away from him. Yet we want nothing to do with people who are mentally sick. It's like talking about corpses. People turn away; they don't like it.

Q: Almost as a counterpoint, there is the repeated intrusion of children into the action of your films. That seems to be a device that Sam Peckinpah uses too, perhaps influenced by your work.

A: Yes, and I love his films. You know, he called me—I've never met him—and offered to do Second Unit on *The Big Red One*. It was a good idea, but it didn't come off. I would have loved that. Anyway, whatever has happened to adults will reflect on children. There is something that gets to me about a child emulating an adult. It is unfortunate if they grow up to be the same kind of sons-of-bitches, and then they presume to pass judgment on a new generation of children. I laugh at that.

Q: In *Shark!*—a film I know you are not happy with—there is a very positive relationship between the child called Runt [Carlos Barry] and Caine, played by Burt Reynolds.

A: I thought it would be interesting to have an adult thief and a child thief working together. I wanted to show, very clearly, the attitude of the adult thief, where, instead of inviting the boy not to steal, he tells him the most important thing is not to get caught. That to me is an editorial about how a lot of people raise children.

I have had the experience of seeing that in life. I have talked to young hoodlums. They told me that they were brought up by other hoodlums, who never tried to differentiate between right and wrong. All the hoodlums try to do is not get caught.

Q: There are often characters named Griff in your films: *The Baron of Arizona, House of Bamboo, Forty Guns, The Naked Kiss,* and *The Big Red One.* Is there a special reason?

A: No, it's that I write a lot of stories and I get sick and tired of trying to change the names. Once I was writing two stories at the same time, and the characters of one appeared in the other. I got all confused, so I said, "Whenever I can, I'll use the same name." It's easier for me to write that way, [though] there is no real Griff. But I'll have to stop it now because I've done it too often. It's just mental laziness on my part.

Q: In your films, there's a lot of physical violence, which might be connected with the fact that you have made Westerns, gangster films, and war films. But you have said that you prefer dramatizing "emotional violence," and you talk about "the bullets of emotion."

A: I don't care too much for physical violence, even though I use it a lot. It's good for many melodramas. That has been proven as far as ticket buyers are concerned. But I prefer "emotional violence." You don't have to be violent with your fist, a voice can do it as well. One word can cut the hell out of your heart.

[There's an] old film I love, written by Noel Coward and directed by David Lean: *Brief Encounter,* with Trevor Howard and Celia Johnston. It has more violence in it—emotional violence—than an automobile chase, or a horse chase, or a fight in a saloon. There is the violence inside the woman who is about to cheat on her husband, and the violence inside the man who is about to cheat on his wife. They are doing something they not only believe is wrong, but something they both reject, even though they are accepting it at the same time. That to me is pure violence, and only once in a thousand times do I find that in a film.

Q: In *Pierrot le fou,* you say, "Film is like a battleground. Love . . . hate . . . action . . . violence . . . death. In one word—emotion."

A: Yes, that encompasses everything. That is all we can write or talk about.

Q: One aspect of your career you haven't really made a film about is filmmaking. Do you have any plan for such a project?

A: No, but if I ever did approach a story about Hollywood, I would do it about the censors. It would rip the hell out of them, and expose them for what they are: parasites, frauds, and hypocrites. I would do a film about what makes a censor a real bluenose, those pious sons-of-bitches who tell you what to do, and what not to do, and how to think, and what to show!

One reason I'm pissed off with them is that, a number of years ago, I ran into one who was trying to sell scripts. He was using the censorship office in Hollywood as an entrée. That to me is a pretty good reflection of what the hell they represent.

Q: In 1964, you wrote: "An artist's hell will always be paved with the skulls of critics and the bones of censors." You avoided mentioning critics in your tirade against censorship. Do you still feel that way?"
A: Yes, though they have to make a living. George Bernard Shaw used to be a critic. When he became a playwright, he wrote a goddamn article about critics—and he tore them apart. I have read some wonderful critiques by writers whose essays are a hell of a lot better than what they were writing about. But there are those critics who just want to get their literary guns off, who want to prove they sleep with the thesaurus and the dictionary. I suppose there's nothing really wrong in all that, whereas I have little patience with the critics who rip off publicity sheets, or take the goddamn copy out of a brochure and write it up. They're taking money under false pretenses, though they are not the major critics usually.

I think any man who wants to be a critic and review films must also love films and want to make them. That is perfectly logical, and I encourage that. A number of ex-critics have become writers and directors in the U.S., and it has happened on a grander scale in Europe, specifically in France, Italy, and even Britain. I am very fond of [British critic] Peter Wollen, for example. I met him in a bar in Edinburgh in 1969. He had film ideas, and I said, "Write them." He and another man [Mark Peploe] wrote a story called *The Passenger* for Michelangelo Antonioni. That makes me very happy. He did something about [his ideas].

I have tremendous respect for a number of critics and writers. To me, a man like Cyril Connolly or Edmund Wilson could cover anything, and I would enjoy what he wrote.

When I was in Germany, a new movie theatre opened in Cologne, and they asked me if I would review a film [playing there]. I said, "No, I don't write reviews," but they said, "You can do any film you want to see." Well, I had never seen *The Ballad of Cable Hogue*, so I said, if they ran that film, I'd write about it. When I saw the film, I realized it was a modern version of Moliere's *Tartuffe*, done very, very well. The other critics in Cologne and Berlin were upset with my review. They only wrote about whether they liked the film. I didn't give a damn about that. I wrote about the cleverness of Tartuffe, a man with one hand under a girl's skirt and the other holding a Bible. I just loved it.

Q: I assume from the fact that you accepted parts in films made by Godard, Luc Moullet, and Wenders, that you admire their work?
A: Yes, very much. Wenders called me again recently and said, "Would you do a walk-on for my new film, *Hammett*?" I said, "Certainly." I really enjoyed [appearing in] it. It's not finished, but so far I'm in it.

Q: Both you and Nicholas Ray were in Wenders's *An American Friend*, but in different scenes.
A: I've known [Nick] a bit for a long time, but we didn't really work together. Wenders was making a film about Ray in New York [*Lightning Over Water*], and he called me and he was crying. He was all choked up and said, "Nick Ray died."

Q: It seems to me that your stories are less concerned with psychologically complex characters, and more with the complexities of situations.
A: It excites me to deal with how society breaks itself down. I try to reflect that on the screen. I don't make up stories about pickpockets, Communists, radicals, reactionaries, they are just reflections of what happens all over the world, in every country. They make very good copy.

Q: You never give much of the history of a character, but deal with how a character acts in the present tense.
A: It's not a question of getting into the character's history, or weaknesses or strengths. I don't like to pinpoint anyone in black and white. Most of us have a hidden side: most of us get away with it, some are caught out. If I ran *Pickup on South Street* for a thousand priests, a thousand ministers, and a thousand rabbis—I am talking about religious people now—I would be interested to know if any of them would have a reflection on what [Richard Widmark's pickpocket] did as a child. Did he steal? Did he lie?

Q: Would you explain what has been described as your "colored chalk" system of planning a film?
A: I have a blackboard and I separate it into three panels for Acts 1, 2, and 3. White chalk just means my storyline. I introduce characters by using yellow chalk. If I have anything "romantic" or "gentle" or "peaceful," I use blue. And for "action," I use red. If I am doing a melodrama, I look at the bottom of Acts 1, 2, and 3, and see if the red increases from 1 to 2, and 2 to 3. If the red does not increase, then I don't have a melodrama.

Q: Do you ever fall in love with your characters?
A: I fall in love with characters I know I'm going to kill off. In *Pickup on South Street*, for example, I fell in love with the character of Moe, played by Thelma Ritter. I knew many Moes. She was a composite of men and women who are police informers. Thelma's dead now, but while we were shooting, I told her how much I loved the character she was playing. And she said, "Look, don't fall in love with me too much, because I love the scene where they blow my head off, and I don't want to lose it."

Q: Is it possible to film what is going on in someone's mind?
A: That's a dream of mine, though it's very difficult. When you go into a restaurant, even as you are saying, "Hello, Pete," in your mind there is something that happened at the office three days ago, and on top of that is what happened in the car while you were driving to the restaurant. Generally, the average human being has a thousand flashes that go through the mind in the time that it takes Pete to say, "How are you, Tom?" and you to say, "I'm okay, Pete." I'd love to get that on the screen.

Q: Your characters relate through the way they bargain with each other, deceive each other. That seems a very cynical attitude toward the human animal.
A: On the contrary, I don't believe I'm a cynic. I am quite an optimist. I might get angry, but there is a big difference between cynicism and anger. I am only a cynic when it comes to the hypocrites' familiar bullshit. They will tell you it's bad to kill, or it's good to show compassion, and then go ahead with their Inquisitions. That's been going on for hundreds of years, from the Spanish Inquisition to now in South Africa, or in Khomeini's Iran. There, one man says, "I'm a good Moslem but you are a bad Moslem because you do not pray on the right knee to Allah." It goes way back to Socrates, nothing has changed.

Q: Why did it take thirty years for *The Big Red One* to come together?

A: It was my fault. I had collected little mementos in Europe during the War—many barns could be wallpapered with newspapers and magazines—but I didn't do anything with them. I would write something down and send it to my mother, giving her the name of the town, the country, the date, and the action. I sent home all kinds of little souvenirs, and she accumulated them over three years, in case I ever wrote a book. But after the War, I did nothing about it. I just kept my two-and-a-half suitcases, which were filled with the stuff.

In 1958, my agent said, "Are you ever going to do a story on the Big Red One?" I said, "Yes." He told John Wayne, and Wayne called me. We had lunch. He said, "I want to be in the film you are going to do about the 1st Division." Wayne acted as my agent and he took me to see Jack Warner. Then he gave the story to Page One of *Variety* and *The Hollywood Reporter*. He even announced the salary he was going to get, which was $77,777.77.

The editor of Bantham Books came to my office and said, "I read in the trades that you are going to do *The Big Red One* with Wayne. Don't do it. Don't do a film, give me a book. I'll get you a hardcover and, a year later, Bantham will come out with a paperback." I liked the idea and told Wayne, but he said, "To hell with the goddamn book, do the film." And Oscar Dystel—he's now the chairman of the board of Bantham—said, "To hell with the film, do the book."

I did neither. Until [many years later, when] Peter Bogdanovich said, "If you write the goddamned script, I'll produce it." And that's what happened. I wrote the goddamned thing, and Peter said, "Who do you want?" I said, "Lee Marvin." He sent it to Lee Marvin, and Marvin phoned me from Tucson, Arizona, and said, "This is your Sergeant."

Peter then took it to Lorimar, while I made three [scouting] trips to Europe and Africa. In the meantime, Peter had a commitment to make a film called *Saint Jack*, about a lovable pimp in Singapore. So Gene Corman became the producer, and we made the film for Lorimar.

Q: Lee Marvin seems to embody the ideal Sam Fuller character.

A: Yeah, he's crazy! It's lucky for him the son-of-a-gun is wearing pants, otherwise I would fall in love with him. We worked together like two goddamn horses pulling the same stagecoach.

Q: The film was originally much longer than its present 113 minutes.

A: The original cut was four hours and twenty minutes. I cut this down to two hours. Then we brought in another editor. I liked 90 percent of his cut. He put back some things I didn't like, but I was happy to have it under two hours. A four-hour film is too much, if you want to get it into a lot of theatres.

Q: Originally, did the film have the voice-over narration by Zab [Robert Carradine]?
A: That was later. They brought in a writer who went through my book [ed.—Fuller's novelization of *The Big Red One*] and took stuff out of it. If the film is successful, Merv Adelson of Lorimar is taken with the idea of rereleasing it in its full length.

Q: You don't think that *The Big Red One* has been defaced by shortening it?
A: No, it couldn't hurt it. I'm not telling a story like the average story-teller. I'm telling the story of three years of war, and people would never miss sequences [they'd never know I had written and filmed]. For every sequence I did use, I could have used twelve or fifteen. There is a magnificent sequence that was cut with my wife, Christa Lang, who played the role of a German countess, and Siegfried Rauch, who plays Schroeder, a German soldier. We shot in Ireland in a big castle. It was beautiful, but slowed down the film.

Q: In 1942, you wrote the novel *The Dark Page*, which was published in 1944, while you were in the Army. Can I connect that with the character of Zab, who writes a book called *The Dark Deadline*?
A: That's legitimate. Zab is me for about three or four little things. One, smoking the cigar. Two, having written a book before he was in the Army. Three, my mother did sell it to a publisher in New York, and I did come across an Armed Services Edition, just as you saw in the film. Also, I made that run on Omaha Beach, when the Sergeant tells them to find the goddamned colonel. Those parts of the Zab character are me.

Q: *The Big Red One* is a war film entirely without heroics.
A: That was the whole idea. The four young [soldiers] are not miracle workers, they are not John Waynes. They are certainly not smarter than anyone else. They are the symbols of the hundreds of thousands of survivors in every army. In war stories, people expect some of the main char-

acters to get killed along the way. There is always someone who gets a letter from his mother and then gets killed. I said, "To hell with that. My [film] will tell the story of four guys who made it."

Q: You have described the film as "a love story between The Sergeant and the four riflemen."
A: Yes, but I didn't want any gushing molasses in there. You have no time to fool around like that in combat. And I tried my best to keep away from the development of young men turning into "men." That's the normal thing in a war film—or in a Western, where a young fellow joins a group hustling cattle, and by the end of the drive he becomes a "man." I kept away from that, because when you are killing, or being killed, there is no time for development of anything, except the drive to live.

Q: What do you see going on inside the head of Griff [Mark Hamill] when he fires the gun repeatedly into the Nazi gas chamber?
A: At first, he is completely ignorant of what the hell he is looking at. I kept my camera on him just long enough for people to realize he has seen a human skeleton in that oven. And by the time he reaches the second and third doors, and sees the SS man, it is the first time he realizes what the hell he is fighting for. Griff is fighting a very evil thing called Kill. That's Hitler, in this particular case. And you cannot sit at a table with Mr. Kill and discuss any deal—that's impossible. You have to resort to his goddamn level and kill his solders and, if possible, kill him. You have to kill Kill. And the idiocy of it, when it is all over, you can't tell who really won, or who really lost.

Q: There's a scene of a firefight in an insane asylum. The style of the shooting is really unlike any other war film. It's more like the surrealism of somebody like Buñuel.
A: I love his work, and what I try to do is get a very coherent and quiet approach to insanity. I didn't want any [patient] yelling or screaming. I didn't want any silly questions asked, with the exception of one: "Is it all right to kill an insane man?" I wanted that done in a very off-the-shoulder way. I kept away from bloodshed, because I don't like ketchup on the screen.

Q: That's a wonderful moment, when the fellow in the asylum grabs a machine-gun and says, "I'm sane, I'm sane, like you!" and proceeds to fire at random.

A: Well, that's your whole theme of sanity and insanity. If they are copying us, who the hell is insane?

Q: That's a disturbing scene, but also very funny. *The Big Red One* seems to have a "fuller" comic sense than your other films. It looks more worked out.
A: I am glad you said that, because the 10 percent of the last cut that I didn't like was the 10 percent without humor.

Q: There's a crazy scene where the Germans, fleeing from an unseen enemy, run into a cave and get mowed down by another unseen enemy, the soldiers hiding there.
A: Yeah, it is funny. Half the time when people are taking a piss on the battlefield, they have no idea of the drama that could be taking place fifteen feet away. We once hid in an area where the Germans were standing above us. They pissed on us, and we couldn't do a thing about it. And one guy began to laugh. There was so much noise that the goddamn son-of-a-bitch who was pissing didn't hear the guy laughing. But imagine if he'd heard him. Imagine the guy with his cock out shooting a rifle. That would have been a hell of a scene, if you know what I mean.

Q: In this film, the Germans seem reflections of the Americans, except on the other side.
A: All human beings are the same once they are on the line with a rifle. The difference here is that we were not brought up to commit mass murder, nor were they in Australia, England, or France. Hitler's was a very precise plan, which he wrote about in detail in *Mein Kampf.* The [orientations] of the German and the American soldiers were different. Once we were on the line with our weapons, we were the same.

Q: Are the soldiers' nicknames in your film reference to soldiers you knew?
A: Yeah. Some are dead and some are still living.

Q: Why does The Sergeant [Lee Marvin] have no other name?
A: Because he is a symbol of war. It doesn't make any difference who he is and where he comes from. He's Death. And without going into a big editorial, when Death meets Death, when he meets the German at the end, nobody really wins. The only reason the Sergeant wants to keep the son-of-a-bitch alive at the end is because it will keep himself alive. And

the definition of the thin line between "to kill" and "to murder" is very important to him.

The hypocrisy of the whole thing is that a piece of paper with a scratch of a pen tells me when I am allowed to kill [you, my interviewer,] Tom Ryan, and when I am not. A son-of-a-bitch thousands of miles away signs a piece of paper. If I was going to kill you, I'd want to kill you because I want to kill you, not because some son-of-a-bitch writes, "It's okay, Fuller, now you can kill Tom Ryan."

Q: What I liked about the film was that it wasn't didactic, it just showed the absurdity of war.
A: Ah, you got it. I didn't have to spell these things out. I went out of my way to make sure that it would be an intimate and very quiet look at a rifle in action. Men in war don't talk about the war. The only thing I remember from three years is not, "What are we doing here?" or "Why are we fighting?" but "Why the hell isn't there somebody here to relieve us?" and "Where is K Company?" and "Where is I Company?"

Q: It's a question of survival rather than comradeship?
A: You are right: "I don't mind if Tom Ryan and the 2nd Platoon gets killed." I am using your name as an example, but that is exactly the dialogue. We would say, "Fuck 'em, they got it. But we made it." Now that is the story of the infantry!

In the action at Omaha Beach, my real sergeant rattled off those numbers just the way Marvin does: number one, number two, number three, number four—just like that. No emotion. That's the overall thing I tried to get in this film—and, as far as women are concerned, I caught it—is the lack of emotion these men had. That to me is the emotion of the entire film.

Q: You have written a novel called *The Rifle* about Vietnam, but it doesn't seem to be available in Australia.
A: It will be published in Flemish. If the goddamn book is slightly successful, I think I will be able to get British, French, and American publishers. My approach is to tell it from the side of the U.S. in Vietnam, and they are right. And to tell it from the side of the Viet Cong, and they are right. And to tell it from the side of Ho Chi Minh, and he is right. They all feel right when they stand in front of a mirror and look at the goddamn reflections in their eyes and do not blink.

The idea at the end is that not only are they all wrong, they are full of shit. All of them. Do China or the Soviet Union or the U.S. really give a goddamn about a little area called Indo-China, that nobody ever heard about until 1954? One says, "I want to give them their freedom," and the other says, "I want to give them their freedom." But both want the crumbs, and they want the cake. That is the story of the book.

Fuller without a Script

Noel Simsolo/1982

From *La Revue du Cinéma*, no. 375 (September 1982): 56–62. Reprinted by permission of Noel Simsolo.

For the opening of his latest film, *White Dog*, Samuel Fuller stayed in Paris for several days. I knew from before that he was a big talker, and I was able to verify that he hadn't changed since our last meeting. It was not an easy interview to lead. Fuller follows his train of thought down to the smallest details. He can dwell for hours on someone that he likes, but just as easily evoke the essence of his work in a single phrase. So, we decided to conserve the unscripted quality of our meeting, instead of summarizing what was said over more than two hours.

The Apotheosis of the Loser

Q: There are never any heroes in your films. The characters are always on the outskirts of society, or "losers."

A: From my first work, I came up against this problem of the "hero." I should show a great guy who helps his mother, who saves the woman he loves. I should witness his struggles against a bad guy, and see that he is rewarded with the girl's love. All that doesn't really interest me. It never interested me. First of all, there are no heroes! There are none anywhere in the world. It's a lie! To believe that inventing heroes like that can add to the drama of a film or book is stupid. I'm happy to accept a "hero" like Clark Gable in *Gone with the Wind*. He's close to my approach to things: he's a son of a bitch who doesn't give a damn about the South, the war, and who uses his brains to make money. I think that he's honest and without any hypocrisy. At the end of the film, he leaves the girl. I love that! In my opinion, that's a marvelous and exciting "hero."

In my first movie, *I Shot Jesse James*, the main character was an assas-

85

sin, a traitor who killed his best friend with a bullet to the back when he was living with him. That's a "hero," good for my stories! I like outcasts, rejects who have to live outside of civilization or society. In *Run of the Arrow* I constructed the story of a bastard of a Southern racist who is against the United States. He would like it if every Yankee on the planet disappeared. That's someone you wouldn't want around! My characters are like that. If they weren't, I wouldn't be interested in them.

Q: But they end up discovering something inside them.
A: Of course! But I want to show you that there's nothing new. When I was at the front, during the Second World War, I wrote a book, *The Dark Page*. Howard Hawks bought the rights to make a movie out of it with Humphrey Bogart and Edward G. Robinson. My mother had to manage the $15,000, because I was still busy fighting the Nazis.

Someone else bought the rights to the book for United Artists, then another producer bought them for Columbia. He paid $100,000. All of that took a lot of time, and then the film got made. Phil Karlson directed it [in 1952] and called it *Scandal Sheet*. I saw the movie, and it was so bad that I left in a laughing fit. They had transformed the main characters into heroes! John Derek and Broderick Crawford acted like heroes. It was ridiculous!

Q: Some people think that not only are your characters racist and fascist, but so are your films.
A: They're wrong! Things get spread around about my films. Going through some old folders, I came upon a bunch of texts that were written around the time of *The Steel Helmet*. Some journalists called me a fascist and other ones accused me of Communism. For the same movie!

Q: You're really more of an anarchist.
A: I love anarchists! But let's get things straight. Whether it's me, you, my mother, my wife, anyone, when we watch a movie, if we think it has political ideologies in it that we disapprove of, we're not going to like the movie. If we agree with the political ideologies, we like the movie. In the first case, we think that the person who made the film is against us. In the second case, that he's on our side. If they're fascists, they'll call me a Communist. And vice versa. It's dumb! Me, I just write a story and I feel passionate about my characters. When I was shooting *China Gate*, someone told me that it was an anti-Communist work. I replied, "It's anti-Communist because it's the story of the commander of the

Indo-China Foreign Legion who fights the Communists. If I had made the story of a Communist group who fights against the Foreign Legion, I would have, according to your logic, made a Communist film." To understand everything, you have to look at the images. I'm telling a story with pictures and sound, not with pamphlets! Throughout *China Gate*, the Chinese Communist is shown to be the only generous, sensible, and intelligent being. He offers to take care of the [Eurasian] girl's child that she had with an American who doesn't want to recognize it. He wants to take her to Moscow so she can escape from the war and racism! He's an ex-teacher who doesn't make a lot of money because teachers don't make a lot of money anywhere in the world. In Moscow, he could become a general and a diplomat because he speaks seven languages, and even Ho Chi Minh only speaks five. He's a really nice guy, and he wants to save this woman and her child. And she kills him! (Fuller bursts out laughing.) Oh, I love that type of story.

Q: In *Pickup on South Street*, the man [Richard Kiley] who's looking for the documents that Richard Widmark stole is a mercenary, and not a militant Communist.
A: He's an agent who offers his services to the highest bidder. The type of guy who lives for money. If I tell him to gather all the information there is about you, and that I'll pay him for it, he'll say okay. If you pay him even more money, he'll give you information about me. He has no ideals. He'll sell his services to anyone. He's like Widmark's pickpocket. They don't give a damn about ideology and patriotism. When critics can't understand that, I lose my cool and my patience.

Q: Changing subjects: you seem to be influenced by German Romantic culture.
A: I don't have any German ancestry, but I understand what you're saying. That could explain the admiration I had for my friend E. A Dupont. I also get along really well with Fritz Lang. I sent him the screenplay for *Straightjacket*, which *Shock Corridor* was later based on. He didn't make the movie, but we met. He's an amazing director, that goes without saying, but he also has a sense of humor. Oh, he's a hell of a guy!

Q: His approach to violence is similar to yours.
A: In my films, the most horrific violence is never shown. It remains between the lines. I manage it with editing and music. Remember in *Underworld U.S.A.*, the [gangland] character [Cliff Robertson] never touches

the people he wants to take down in revenge. He turns them against each other, or over to the FBI. He doesn't hit them, and he doesn't take his revenge directly. That's an interesting type of violence!

Q: You also like German music.
A: I love all kinds of music. I've worked with some great composers like Victor Young and Paul Dunlap. I've also used Beethoven. When I was young, I had a record player that could automatically change records, and a Brahms movement was followed by a Haydn movement, followed by a Beethoven concerto, and so on. I realized: it all worked together! I applied this discovery of musical collage to my films, like the beginning of *Verboten!* I like when the music changes during the same scene. When I listen to music, I think of the composer writing emotions, and I imagine stories. I visualize everything. It's up to me to transmit [what I visualize] to the audience.

A Consul Named Romain Gary

Q: Could we talk about *White Dog*?
A: That's a whole story in itself. I'd read that novella by Romain Gary. It was published in *Life* more than ten years ago. But I have to tell you how I knew Romain Gary. He was French consul in Los Angeles and he contacted me in 1958 to get together for lunch. During the meal, he told me that he had been a pilot in the War. I had also fought in the War and we talked about that. Then he came to the point. The lunch was a diplomatic strategy. He said to me, "You made a film about war for Fox. The one called *China Gate*. I love that movie and I understand what it's talking about. BUT . . . but, there's a prologue to the film, with an illustrated commentary of documented German, French, and Japanese war strategies. That commentary is horrifying. The images, too: desolation, death, buildings in flames and bombed ruins. I want to ask you to remove this 'preface.'" Because Gary worked for the French government, his arguments were those of a diplomat. I told him, "I cannot, sir, remove these images because I am not the one who filmed them. If I had filmed them, I could remove them. But I want to tell you that these French war planes for Indo-China that you find shocking are planes that were filmed by the French news." That's what happened: I went to see French documentaries and I saw terrible things.

Gary lowered his head and muttered: "I know that very well." I asked Gary, "What if it had been Italian footage?" He said: "Then it wouldn't have bothered me." Ha! What a guy!

I read a book that he wrote in 1949: *The Company of Men*. It tells the story of surviving children just after the War. It's a marvelous book. Me, I never buy the rights to books, I write my own stories, but Gary's agent asked me to talk to [Darryl F.] Zanuck about it. This agent thought that Zanuck would buy it, and I could write the screenplay. Anyway, Gary had lunch with me and he said, "There are only two people in this world who like that book: you and me. You've talked so enthusiastically about it to me. Why don't you make it into a movie?" I responded, "Because I've already seen the movie." He choked, "That's impossible. I never sold the rights to anyone!" I watched him going crazy. I told him, "I've seen [Vittorio] De Sica's *Shoeshine*. It's a great movie, and it's the same story. In De Sica's film, the children turn their backs on one another to count their money in secret. It's fantastic because you see that they had to grow up so fast, and they're like old Dickens's misers. In your book, the kids collect condoms, wash them, clean them, repackage them, and resell them. It's amazing! But if I tell that story, everyone is going to think of *Shoeshine!*"

Q: And *White Dog*?
A: Finally, I'm getting to *White Dog*. After having read it, I had a conversation with Gary. "That a white person could be such a bastard that he would train a dog to kill blacks, that's really strong," I told him. "But that the black guy retrains the dog to attack whites, that doubles the crime, and makes it into a racist story!" That was the wrong basis for a story. That's what Paramount had been struggling with for years.

Gary had, with this story, written an allegory. It all had to do with his relationship with his wife, Jean Seberg, [and she with the Black Panthers]. Paramount didn't know that. They bought the rights, and made seven or eight adaptations out of it. Robert Evans wanted to produce it for Roman Polanski. Then they were thinking of Arthur Penn, of Don Siegel, etc. Everyone was struggling to make the adaptation because they didn't understand that it was an allegory, like Homer's, or Defoe's *Robinson Crusoe*, which is nothing but a book against Great Britain. And then, it was Jon Davison who wanted to produce it. He had just had colossal success with *Airplane!*, a movie that made many hundreds of thousands of dollars. Davison agreed to take care of producing if I was the one to direct it. I'd never even met the guy! When all of that was decided, I was in Buenos Aires.

When I arrived home in LA, Christa, my wife, was waiting for me at the airport. She told me that Davison had called, and said to remind me that he'd sent me a fan letter two years before. He told her that he was coming to our house in two days, with the head of Paramount. They were going to pitch a film to me. I told my wife that it was all impossible. I had a contract with CBS, they'd paid me for a script, and I was supposed to go and start staking out locations in Japan. Even if they offered me the story of Mary Magdalene, descending from the heavens to meet [Menachem] Begin, it was impossible. Christa said to me, "It's *White Dog!*" That changed things. We went home and I read the script they had sent me. Paramount had already spent a million dollars on the script, and it was still not at a point where we could shoot it.

When they got to my place, I explained that I wasn't available, but that the script relied on a bad idea. They could write fifty scripts. It would still be a racist film. I added, "I'll give a solution to you for free because Gary was my friend. You have to invent a scientist, a black guy, who wants to reconfigure the dog's brain to rid it of that component. No more of this making him attack whites instead of blacks! The man is a scientist who works with animals. He's already tried several times to heal this kind of dog. He wants a 100 percent successful result." The head of Paramount started shouting, "That's it! A black scientist! Make the film!" But I was working on a film about terrorism for CBS. An $8 million budget! He told me he would work things out with the head of CBS. Later, the head of CBS called me in and asked why I absolutely wanted to make *White Dog*. I said to him, "I know the man who wrote the book." He replied, "OK. That's a good enough reason for me." And I started to work on the script.

Q: *White Dog* draws on themes that are of personal interest to you. The characters, including the dog, are driven by fixations.
A: Yes, they're wearing blinders. They only pay attention to their obsessions. The dog, too. I directed him like a human being. It was an attack dog. There was a signal for him to pounce. You had to be careful on the set because the slightest noise that sounded like the signal could make him attack . . . me! I talked to him like an actor. Did you notice the close-ups of his eyes in the film? I looked him right in the eye. I wanted the dog to be shown as a thinking being. Me, I hate movies like *Lassie*.

Q: You can tell the dog is thinking when he understands how to get out of the gate. The editing is fantastic.
A: You saw that! That's great. Really, I'm thrilled about that because a film's language counts everything for me. And I like mixing in bits of documentary with bits of fiction.

Q: When the dog kills the black man in the church, you have a stained-glass window showing St. Francis sitting with a white dog.
A: That's irony. It's a critique of religion. Christ wants to save all people, but he only has success one at a time. He didn't see the big picture! The dog has the same disability.

Q: When the three characters leave the traveling circus, after the dog's death, they are, in my eyes, three symbols of "loserdom." Three societal rejects: a black man, an actress, and an old white man.
A: Exactly! They're outcasts, pariahs. They leave the film as failures. They didn't look at the big picture. They were only paying attention to their fixations. You know, those are the kind of characters that I love!

An Interview with Sam Fuller

Don Ranvaud/1982

From *Framework* 19 (1982): 26–28. Reprinted by permission of Don Ranvaud.

Don Ranvaud interviewed Samuel Fuller during the Salsomaggiore Film Festival in Italy, 1982.

DR: A lot of things started in Edinburgh. Did the rediscovery of your films at the Edinburgh Fest cause you to change your attitudes to cinema, to make you more self-conscious?

SF: Yes. But I would call it discovery rather than rediscovery because I had never had any kind of accolade before then. When I was invited to Edinburgh, [the Scottish filmmaker] Murray Grigor was there, [programmer] Linda Myles, [critic] Peter Wollen, [critic] Kingsley Canham, and people like that. From Edinburgh Ken Wlaschin called from the London Film Festival, and they went ahead [in London] and did the same thing. Books were written and I became a kind of celebrity to a point where I had to take all the mirrors out of the house where I lived because it went to my head! Seriously, it was a wonderful feeling and I now know how Shirley Temple must have felt. All round I would say that I owe the [Edinburgh Festival] anything that is in connection with making a dollar or being "bankable."

Edinburgh reminds me of a story I want to make which Murray Grigor was very anxious to produce. I have a story about Dick and Brody, I mean the real Dick and Brody . . . one hundred years before Robert L. Stevenson was born there was Dick and Brody, the man with two lives. That inspired Stevenson to write *Dr. Jekyll and Mr. Hyde*. One day I would like to make this story in Edinburgh, the old Edinburgh down by Dean Bridge with its atmosphere—a certain type of cobblestone streets and gallows and everything else connected with locksmiths and executions.

DR: Your attitude to women is very ambiguous. Some think that you have managed to make birth a male experience in *The Big Red One*'s tank. On the other hand, women like your pictures a lot because the women characters have "balls," as you would say.

SF: Well, I did not set out deliberately to have anything to do with a feminist feeling. I did it from a character viewpoint and no matter what the picture is, I thought it would be a very good idea to have a woman as the heavy, a villain—rough. In other movies, it would be a man like Edward Arnold or Claude Rains fighting an idealist, a Jimmy Stewart or a Gary Cooper. I made the woman the heavy and not the romantic little girl like in a [John] Wayne picture, where she waves the cavalrymen off and cries when they return. Women loved my idea. Women in my pictures became an entity, there was no discussion about breasts, about ass, or about sex . . . nothing. Another example: *Forty Guns*, a thriller about someone in the American West after the Civil War who collected taxes for the United States. He kept most of the money, figuring that if he collected a thousand dollars, kept nine hundred and sent one hundred to Uncle Sam, that's a hundred dollars he never would have seen. Generally you have a man doing that, but I thought it would be good to have a woman—[Barbara] Stanwyck played the part. Again, the women loved it. I love the whole idea of any women on the screen having balls because generally they *do* have balls. Unfortunately *man's* rule and *man's* beliefs, not the Lord's, have made them the inferior sex and subjected them to slavery in a form without any stripes, in a jail without any cells. That's why I'm nutty about any situation in which a woman has big balls and waves them and makes a noise like the clanging of two big shells in bells on any street.

DR: You say that you did not set out deliberately to have anything to do with feminism but you do have strong feelings about the position of women in society.

SF: A woman is a slave, a chattel, she is owned by a man. Because she gives birth to a child, it's the only thing she has been deemed good for, for thousands of years. Now that is wrong. A woman is a human being just like a man, a woman should have the same rights, women are entitled to equality in every phase of life. When equality in all laws and in every nation is talked about, it's always in terms of men, including in the United States. The Declaration of Independence says that all *men* are created equal, it doesn't say *men and women*. In the United States up until

1926 an American woman who married a foreigner lost her citizenship. In 1926 a law was passed . . . oh, isn't that a beautiful law! An American woman marries a foreigner and does not lose her citizenship. The hypocritical irony of that is that even in the 1920s we had this law, and its repeal is just another example of tokenism. We now have women judges, a woman governor, but they are like tokens, it's like using a black man as a judge, an actor, a director, it is called token—*TOKEN*. It's not sincere. Women's rights should not come from speeches or laws, or parades with pickets, that's bullshit, good but bullshit. What's not bullshit is if every man says, goddamnit I'm not better. That is the way I feel about it.

DR: How did you come to be involved in the *White Dog* project?

SF: First of all *White Dog* has nothing to do with the color of the animal. *White Dog* is the definition of a dog trained by a bigot since a puppy to grow up and attack blacks. The way these Ku Klux Klanners and members of the White Citizens' Council trained people to grow up and hate anyone who is black and anyone with contrary religious beliefs. The original story was written by Romain Gary about twelve years ago, it appeared in *Life* magazine in its entirety, and they gave him the cover as well. Romain Gary wrote an allegory or parable which was an autobiography of his own life, the life of his wife, Jean Seberg, and the Black Panthers situation. As you know, Jean Seberg took her own life, and soon afterwards Romain Gary did the same. When Paramount bought the story seven or eight years ago it was for Robert Evans to produce and Roman Polanski to direct. Since, they have had seven or eight scripts—then I was called in. Jon Davison, the successful young producer of *Airplane!*, said he would not make the picture unless I wrote and directed it and that's how I met him.

DR: In order to be a good filmmaker, or make a good film, one has to be a "good cannibal," would you agree?

SF: Yes, 100 percent, in that form and on those terms. Do you want an example? Wim Wenders recently made a film called *The State of Things*. The film is about a movie crew at work on location until there is no money and they stop production, which is where the cannibalism sets in. The director of the film, played by Patrick Bauchau, goes to Hollywood to look for the producer and find out what has happened to the money. Wim then concentrates on the crew and the actors waiting for the producer. If this were not called *The State of Things* it could be called "Waiting for Godard," the director, or "Waiting for Beckett," the producer, or "Waiting for Righty" instead of "Lefty" by [Clifford] Odets. The cannibalism which starts amongst the members of the crew behind the camera and the actors in front is symbolic of life in general covering every emotion from avarice, sensuality, to regret. I haven't seen the film, it's [maybe] opening at Cannes. I play the cameraman, a member of the crew, loosely based on Joe Biroc—a real cameraman who worked with me on a number of pictures. Wim had many artistic touches and I like his tempo—a European tempo, that to me is a superior tempo.

If you make any scenes with violence, [that tempo] is excellent: Fritz Lang's *M*, and the explosive response to the child molester. The cannibalism and cannibalization which takes place [in *M*] amongst the thieves and underworld of Berlin in order to make sure they catch the child killer, so that the cops will leave them alone, takes place among the crew in *The State of Things*. How they eat each other and devour each other! If the actors come up to par with what [Wenders] had in mind, I think he will have a piss cutter of a picture.

DR: But I was also referring to the emotional drain involved with production that rests on a form of cannibalism.
SF: Now that is the mental form. It's not 100 percent strain but it's a drain, it drains the blood, the ambition, the plans, the dreams out of everyone. People snap at each other. It's like being entombed in a prison where you enjoy what you are doing, you don't want it to come to an end. But the monotony, the repetition, the waiting for shots can unnerve you, and you become cannibalistic in your approach. It's a highly charged emotional situation when you live together on location. It's different from being on stage, at least there you can go home every night, here you're stuck together. The word cannibalism is an excellent word, it can mean mental, it can mean physical, or cultural, or spiritual.

DR: Which film do you feel closest to today?
SF: Script-wise my favorite picture was a complete failure when it came out, *Park Row*, because it was a nostalgic picture about a generation I never experienced. It was about people who lived a hundred years before I was born, but it's also about a street which I grew up in. I love newspapers and, until I was thirteen, fifteen, that was my dream [job]. When I was seventeen, I was a crime reporter. By the time I was twenty-two, twenty-three, I found out that it was all a lot of bullshit and so I lost my goddamn interest in being a newspaperman. You have to die poor when you're a newspaperman. But I still love the history of journalism, and *Park Row* is my favorite picture.

The story takes place in 1886 and I had a travelling shot of a man walking down the street and he passes the newspaper offices. Karl Marx worked for the *New York World*, and when the man passes the *World*, I put in a big photograph of Karl Marx with the beard. The people in the crew thought it was one of the Smith Brothers, who made cough drops! Only one editor, Cameron of the *San Francisco Chronicle*, recognized Marx in the picture.

DR: What importance do you give to the script?

SF: Almost 100 percent are my original scripts. The script is something I love to do, whether they like it or not, whether it is good or bad. I am in love with it, and it is the star of any picture I make. If a famous actor can play it, I am very happy, if he cannot play it, I'd use you, my boy . . . it makes no difference. You would be right for the part I thought of early in the morning. Nobody is with me at five or six in the morning when I'm typing, it's my baby. The story is the most important thing in anything, be it a film, a play, or a book. I like to tell stories. Unfortunately, today making a movie has become too big, so that you now have over a hundred people in a crew. The fortunate part is that if you have a crew of five thousand or twenty, the people who pay to see a movie don't give a damn how much it cost or how many people worked in it. They want to know what the story is about. The script is the czar of the whole goddamn film world.

DR: I would have thought *Underworld U.S.A.* may have been a "favorite" of yours—or maybe it's just one of mine . . .

SF: Every time the underworld took one hundred dollars or one million dollars that meant no taxes for Uncle Sam. That made the politicians very unhappy, it made me very happy—that is why I wanted to make the film. Actually I'd like to be in the underworld to make three million, four million, ten million dollars . . . ha . . . ha . . . ha, and say, "Good morning" to the President. I used real names from every department of gangsterism. I met some of the men and I liked them, I liked them a lot more than many of the political people I met. I knew where they stood, and generally I found that most of them were very honorable men except to the people they killed and robbed. I met the head of Columbia, and I suggested using the most famous character in the past two hundred years for adventure. I told him the story of the Count of Monte Cristo and how the young Count was betrayed by three men, and how he got revenge. You are familiar with the Dumas book, *The Count of*

Monte Cristo? That is *Underworld U.S.A.* It was not quite the film I wanted to make. I had to leave out the amount of money made and the names of the men involved making that money. But it was very successful in the United States for, even though I only touched on crime, it was responded to by the newspaper people [across] the nation. I don't want you to go around thinking that I make up stories [saying] that crime does pay. I didn't make that up—out of one hundred crimes committed only two or three are actually solved. I thought it would be very funny if a young man uses the FBI to avenge himself and find the killers of his father, that is why I made that picture.

DR: Your films have been accused of being imperialist and politically reactionary.

SF: When I make a film I am not interested in the political climate, I am interested in the climate as far as the character is concerned. I'll give you an example. I made a war picture many years ago called *The Steel Helmet.* I was on the front page of *The People's World* and the *Daily Worker* who suggested that the film was financed by [General] MacArthur. The Hearst labor columnist Victor Riesel also wrote about the movie. I didn't read it but my mother did, and she rang me in New York and said: "Good morning, Comrade, how are you?" and proceeded to read [to me] the article. Riesel said that this man must be investigated, that he had turned my name over to the Pentagon for making a picture which has a United States soldier shoot down an unarmed prisoner of war, a Manchurian major in Korea. The minute this happened, the men who put up the money said, "Well, we have a controversial hit."

I had an idea of a picture about Russia at the time of the Cold War in 1952 called *Red Square* but we couldn't get anyone in the country to make it. I wanted to do twenty-four hours in the life of a Russian soldier. The minute the picture was announced, they said that I was a radical. When you take a contemporary political subject, the easiest thing to do is to make a propaganda film, to make a picture that interests you from a political situation and not a human situation. If I had made a picture of Stalin in Russia before the War, the capitalist would say that I am a Communist, a fanatic, but everyone in Russia would say I'm a hero.

When some people call my pictures "imperialistic," it makes me laugh. I don't make my pictures anti or pro anything political. If my character is involved, say I make a picture about a Russian spy who is double-crossed by everybody in the United States, that doesn't mean *I'm* a Communist or pro-Communist or anti-American, it means my *character* doesn't like the United States. If you do want to make a film about your political philosophy, you must not make a film for your friends, you must not make a film where everybody who believes ideologically the way you believe will see it. You must make a film that the enemy will see, the people who don't believe what you believe in, if you *really* believe it.

DR: But surely you cannot separate what you call the human from the political?

SF: OK. Let me give you an example. When I was very young I knew some newspapermen who were very friendly with Ezra Pound. I read his Cantos. Some I understood, some I didn't, but what I did understand I liked very much. As years went by, Ezra Pound became a traitor in the United States, lived in Italy, worked for Benito Mussolini, and made speeches for fascism. Being an American I would say, "My God, he's a son-of-a-bitch." I began to think of his Cantos in terms of his politics. Only when he wrote them, they were not political—that's the mistake I made. I then read them and didn't like them, but I was wrong. What he believed in, that was his own business, even if he *was* wrong. It is somebody else's business, if he's wrong, to either change his mind or kill him . . . that's politics. Now I look back on Ezra Pound from an artistic point of view. You should never let the political situation interfere with the character you are writing about. Never.

DR: In 1957 you made a film about Vietnam called *China Gate*. What do you think of recent treatments of the subject, particularly *Apocalypse Now*?

SF: I liked *Apocalypse*. John Milius wrote the screenplay and was going to direct it, but there was a change of plan. However, we lost a war, we invaded [Vietnam] and we lost. I wanted somebody to say that we had lost, but America is a new country and we are not used to defeat. I like both Coppola and Milius, I like them and I like their work. Coppola's work is socially on one side of the rainbow, Milius has worked on the reactionary side of the rainbow. It's immaterial to me. You know, in 1967 I wrote a book and a screenplay about Vietnam told by a twelve-year-old Viet Cong soldier. His god is Ho Chi Minh, his godfather is General Diap, who defeated the French at Dien Bien Phu. The whole war is told through the eyes of the boy. I did nothing with the book until last year when I met a man called Walter Soethoudt, a publisher in Brussels, who was interested in the book. I told him that he wouldn't publish it because it is against every country in the world. No country cares about a place called Laos, Cambodia, or Vietnam. It's a little piece of the cake, it doesn't mean anything. He published the book, it's called *The Rifle*, and it is doing very well now in Belgium. In the book, I detail all the actions of every nation involved in Indo-China, their indifference to it, and all the horror which means nothing to them because they are not involved in all the horror. At the opening of the novel, the little boy sees a plane in the air and his mother and father thrown out of it without parachutes. If this book is any success at all, I'll hear what all the political people have to say about it. I don't think that they will publish it in America and I don't think they will publish it in France. If this book does come out, it'll give anybody a pretty good idea of how I feel about getting involved in something emotionally and then doing nothing about it.

A Long Chat with Sam Fuller

Richard Schickel/1982

Previously unpublished interview. Printed by permission of Richard Schickel.

Q: How did you get into movies from being a newspaperman?

Fuller: I never thought I'd be in the picture business, number one, ever. Though I loved movies . . . Tom Mix and William S. Hart. When I was a kid, I always tried to figure out how Tom Mix had that big hat on in a fight. I saw him go through a glass window and jump off a cliff with [his horse] Tony. There's the water, they get a close-up shot, and his hat is on. I don't know. I didn't understand it.

I was on an unsolved murder [in 1931] that inadvertently got me [noticed by] the movie business. It was a double homicide, my byline, page one, and I got a letter from Loews Incorporated in New York [which owned MGM]. It was perfumed, evidently the secretary, and they said, "We love your story. If you give us an ending—since no one had solved the murder—we'll pay you $5,000."

I went home, my mother said, "Take the five. You'll never see $5,000 in your life. This is it." But I turned it down. I don't want to go into detail, but it was very difficult to solve a murder in New York City, especially when a victim is a multi-millionaire. If he has no family, seven years after his death, the City takes that money . . . and just put that together!

So I was traveling back and forth on newspapers covering different ways of execution: Texas by the gunshot, Oklahoma and Utah hanging, the West Coast electric chair. This led to movies. I met a man in Cicero, outside of Chicago [who owned a billiards club], and I slept on the pool table. I was waiting for Shainmark of the *Chicago-American*, who'd said, "You come out here. We got a spot for you." A small, bald-headed, stocky man came in and asked for directions, the quickest way to go to Chicago. I said, "Can you give me a lift? I'm going to try to get a job on a newspaper, *The Chicago-American*."

In the car, he said, "I know Mr. Shainmark. Ezekial Isaiah Shainmark." I said, "He's a very good editor." He said, "Listen, what did you do before?" I said, "I was on [*The New York*] *Journal*, and on [*The New York Evening*] *Graphic*." He connected me with the double murder, because they were hot murders, very hot. And he said, "Listen, why don't you write for me? I am Herbert Yates, and I am Consolidated Film Company. I also own Republic Studio. We have two stars, Gene Autry and John Wayne." We pulled into Chicago and to the Morrison Hotel. Mr. Yates said, "I'll get you a room here. You write a story for me. Anything. What kind of typewriter do you use?" I said, "Royal. All black ribbon."

The next morning, I gave him my story and he sold it. And he gave me $10,000. It was called *Gangs of New York* [1938]. It's what would happen if Al Capone was said to be sprung, but they keep him as a prisoner, unbeknownst to anyone except the Attorney General of the United States. They have a man who's been scarred and had surgery who's been mimicking him, a phony Al Capone who gets out of jail. There's a big shootout at the end, the men kill "Capone," but they don't know which is the real one.

The minute that was sold, I went to San Diego to the *Sun*, a Scripps-Howard newspaper. And from there to the *LA Herald*. And Yates said, "Do you have anything else? Quick. Give me whatever you want." I said, "What about Typhoid Mary, and the little boy selling newspapers? The kid doesn't know he has typhus. And everyone who buys a paper gets it, you see." He said, "Great!" So they made *Bowery Boy* [1940]. I got a lot of calls [for film stories] while I was on newspapers. They were easy to write and had nothing to do with a big head, or art.

I ran into a very big agent called Charlie Feldman. He said, "We'll give you assignments. But no name." I said, "That's perfectly all right. I don't care about that." My love was a byline in a newspaper. Watching people in the subway read my story. I wrote these ghosted film stories [for Feldman]. I got very good money.

Charlie was drafted, but I didn't want to go in because there was no action. That was pre–Pearl Harbor, and I was writing a book [*The Dark Page*]. But if we were attacked, I'd fight. Otto Preminger was the last one [for whom I wrote anonymously]. He said, "Listen, you don't have to carry a rifle." I said, "If there's a war, I don't want to do anything but. It's the biggest story since William the Conqueror." And I went to war.

Q: Back from the War, didn't you have trouble selling scripts to studios because they were too pessimistic?

A: They said, "We like the writing, we don't like the content." L. B. Mayer didn't love my stories because "Crime does pay." He said, "Boys can't grow up like that." A producer named Robert L. Lippert said to me, "I agree with the studios. It's ridiculous having these kinds of stories. Everybody betraying, and all the bad people in the end living very happily and rich to ninety-five years old." But he said, "I like the way you write." I said, "I want to do the story of Cassius. What makes an assassin an assassin? Is it his idea, or his mother's, his colleague's, his son's, his daughter's?" He said, "That sounds great. But who is Cassius?" And I told him. He said, "You mean the fellows hanging around those Roman baths with those kind of tablecloths they wear? Well, I don't want to touch anything like that."

I went through three or four [other] assassinations, including the President of France. And he said, "We're getting nowhere. I don't like those kinds of periods." I said, "Well, the last resort . . . Robert Ford. He's the guy who shot Jesse James." Lippert jumped up. "We got a picture!" We made a deal, and he mentioned a figure. I said, "That's too much, too much, for the first script." He said, "That's not for the script. That's for the whole movie. Ten days." I said, "I'll do it on the condition I [also] direct, because my mother laughs on the phone every time I write a script and nobody makes the picture." Lippert said, "You can direct it." *I Shot Jesse James* [1948] was made for $104,000. And it was ten days. That was Lippert's personal money. He didn't go to a bank.

Q: You'd gone from the news desk to directing a Hollywood film.
A: I didn't know anything about shooting it. But one thing I learned from newspapers, when a man kills another man and then dies and you look at the two corpses, you'll never be able to determine who is the best of them, or who is a killer. So I began *I Shot Jesse James* with faces, and they're sweating. I didn't want people to know who is the clerk and who is the thief, who is the robber. No, no, no, no, no. And I learned the power of the camera. It's exactly like boldfaced type. And I learned I could milk [a scene] as long as I wanted to: a man with a gun, hands up, lights up. Now you're beginning to know it's a holdup. You don't know you're in a bank. Within the next four or five shots, you know it. I learned something I tried to pass on. Show it! Two little words. It's better than five hundred words of discussion. So that's the beginning of my adventures in Hollywood.

Q: You have a lot of sympathy for the Robert Ford character. It's a real twist on what you expect from this story.

A: I'm glad you said that. You make me happy. Now Jesse is no hero at all. Ever! He and his brother, Frank, the first job they had—I have the newspaper—they held up a hospital military train, robbed the wounded and killed them. That's number one. Number two, when Jesse was sixteen, he was a girl impersonator. I've got the picture of "the House of Love." He would dress as a girl, he would entice soldiers in there, get them drunk, and Frank would kill them. Now I ended my picture in a way like that, where the man who killed Jesse is dying. And he says, and this is to me what was *in* Jesse, "I'm sorry what I done to Jesse. I loved him." And Lippert said, "That's great! I like that kind of relationship like, you know, John Wayne and Ward Bond." And I laughed like hell.

At one time I thought of doing that picture about the sixteen-year-old Jesse. But I didn't want to break any bubble. If I were a kid, I wouldn't want to see Jesse James like that.

Q: The motivation of the Ford character is very simple and pure. He thinks if he kills this guy, he'll get an amnesty. He'll make a few dollars, there's this girl, so maybe they can go get a farm. He hasn't really thought it out. This girl who's an actress probably doesn't want to live on a farm. It's almost a perverse simplicity that the man has, a willed-in capacity to never think more than one step at a time.

A: He's just a poor farmer who happens to be a bank robber. It all makes sense to him, in his apish way of thinking. It's like he'd do anything for the girl, and it's all right [to kill Jesse]. Everything he did was from the heart. And to settle down. That's Horatio Alger, from poor to riches.

Q: Ford didn't think through what would happen if you killed a mythic figure. That you yourself would be the next target, like the confrontation with the young boy.

A: I cast a little kid who looked like him, John Ireland. The little kid takes a shot, and [Bob Ford] starts shooting back at the burst of the gun. The little boy says, the most famous line to me, "Please don't shoot. I'm out of bullets." [It could be:] "Don't shoot, I'm out of a sword. A stone. A club. A javelin." That's what I wanted to get in: the hypocrisy of all people, when they're armed, they never say, "Don't shoot." They shoot. Bob Ford asks, "What the hell did you shoot me for?" He says, "You shot Jesse James. That makes you the biggest gunfighter in the world."

Q: The beginnings of your movies have to be the best of anybody's. *The Steel Helmet*: you think it's a dead man's helmet and then the guy appears out of it. I think of Rod Steiger and *The Run of the Arrow*, where's he's eating lunch off the guy he thinks he's killed. The opening of *The Naked Kiss* is fabulous. I have the feeling that your openings go back to your journalism. I mean, they're great tabloid leads, very vivid.

A: You hit it. They're leads. They usually used bold-faced type on the *New York Journal* for a page-one homicide. And the editor would say, "Hit it as hard as you can [in the lead] because that's the story. The rest, details, they can go on page 30." That taught me a lesson. It's easy to open a picture by establishing a character doing something, but I like to be gripped right away. You don't have to show the city of New York, and you don't have to show buildings, and the waterfront. [Better,] a woman [comes into the frame]. You pull back, and you're seeing things through the sight of a rifle. And you come right to the finger, and he pulls the finger, and wham! There's an explosion way over there. You don't have to see who the hell he hits.

So when you say you like the openings—I'm very happy you like them. But it's not just a trademark. It's from instinct. I'm very impatient when a picture opens up with an establishing shot of where you are, and somebody drives up and he gets out of a car, and he walks to an apartment and he rings the bell, and he goes upstairs and asks, "Is Joe here?" And Joe isn't here. So he goes out. Why didn't he phone? We have telephones.

Q: Your openings plunge you into the story.

A: The heat of the story is what I'm interested in. As the heat get hotter, you begin to see where you are, who is what, and what they are doing. Then you move in closer and closer, and over a shoulder.

Q: That's well put. Let's talk about the sergeant in *The Steel Helmet*. I know you admire people of this kind because he comes back with the Lee Marvin character in *The Big Red One*. He's incredibly competent at what he does, but he's also crazy, isn't he?

A: That's not one character. It's a composite of a few sergeants. They're all similar mentally. You have to have a screw loose, a little bit, to be a squad leader. I was an assistant squad leader, a corporal. But I had no command. He has command. A sergeant of a rifle squad, he says, "Go over behind that rock." He's with it, he's in it, he has to be a little bit weirdo. If you don't do [what he orders], he'll shoot you. If you don't do it NOW! It's so fast. And your head is blown off! A fire fight lasts two or three minutes, that's all. Twenty minutes is unusual. People die very quickly. People are wounded very quickly.

I never saw heroic acts in three years [in the War.] You do something out of instinct because we are animals. You do something to save your life, and while you are saving your life, you save three other lives, and while you are doing the same, you save 150 lives, á la Sergeant York. Now because of Washington, there's the Purple Heart, the Silver Star. It never dawned on us about being a hero. I'm against war to such an extent! Don't forget, the average professional soldier is the most anti-war person in the world.

So we get back to the sergeant in *The Steel Helmet*. He's a professional soldier. He's not too dumb, not too brilliant. But there's a cunning about this man that I try to catch. And he has an armor about him, and kids mean nothing. His mother would mean nothing. Survival means everything. That's all. That's the man.

Because he blew his top and killed the Commie [POW in cold blood], the [US] government got very upset, and my mother called me from New York, and she said, "Hello, comrade." I'll never forget it. "What happened?" She said, "You are an un-American, anti-American Communist." It was [a piece] written by Victor Riesel, a syndicated labor columnist. He said, "This is the most un-American, and this is. . . ." I should be investigated. Under reviews of *The Steel Helmet*, Riesel wrote a whole column, and, the next day, another column. "Who is this fellow? Who made this picture? An American! He makes a beast out of the American soldier, who shoots down the very small. He has a big fellow as a sergeant, and a very thin little Chinese Communist officer he killed. Where is the killing? In a Buddhist temple!"

Q: I assume you disagreed with Riesel's analysis?
A: It's against the law to shoot a prisoner-of-war, an unarmed man? What law? That's all hooey. The law is a young man with a rifle. That's the law.

Now, *The People's World* and the *Daily Worker* had me on page one: "Magnificent! Except the last half of the picture." They said, "The last half was financed by General MacArthur." And a famous French critic, George Sadoul, tore me apart, that "[Fuller] said something against Communism, he's a reactionary." I found out that he was a professional Lefty.

It was a very controversial picture. I have a scene where the [Korean POW] says to a Nisei, a second- or third-generation Japanese American soldier, "Why do you fight along with these white son-of-a-bitches? I heard they had put-'em-away places and all that in the War." And the Nisei says, "They're camps. My mother was put away in a camp in Arizona, my father in California." That's on the screen, a taboo statement. It's real, but I'm not ashamed of it. Our country's only two hundred years old. What the hell! We should never do it again is better than feeling ashamed.

Q: The movie actually did well in the theatres.
A: I got a call from [Columbia head] Harry Cohn, and he said, "It won't work. No girls. And you have one set and only a few men." When the picture went out, it got great reviews and made a lot of money. Big money. Cohn bought theatres with that money. He said, "Well, I was wrong." I said, "The stories I used are real news stories. Prisoners of war were killed. They did put civilians in camps in the United States. That's real." I tried to get as close as possible to the roughness without exaggeration. This is not a tough guy from Victor McLaglen's tough guy in *What Price Glory?* These are not tough guys that sit around and talk about the women and drinking, and go into bars and fight, you see? The average soldiers in my outfit, a division of fifteen thousand men, were clerks and truck drivers and insurance men, young delivery men. That's what they were.

Q: In *The Steel Helmet*, there's the protagonist and a little kid who attaches himself to the man, and a relationship develops. Usually in your films, the guy tries to push a kid away, but somehow the kid worms his way in. It's in *Shark!*, it's in a lot of your pictures.
A: Before you take an area in war, you clobber it with bombs and artillery shells. The only thing you'll find [after] are old men and women who couldn't make it out, dead animals, or a living child, abandoned in all that confusion. We always had a kid somewhere, coming out of the rubble. That to me is the only contact we have with the civilians we fight. Every infantryman has that everywhere. Children forgotten. Orphans. That's why I like a kid in the picture. In *The Big Red One*, they find a kid. He's pulling his dead mother to the beach so she can be buried. He won't tell them where his secret German gun is until they promise him a four-handle casket.

Q: *Fixed Bayonets* (1951) is about a guy, Denno [Richard Basehart], who is an assistant squad leader, and he's terrified he'll have to take over the squad and may actually shoot somebody. Is that character a projection of your emotions in wartime?

A: We all felt like that. This man couldn't kill face to face. He just couldn't. And when he does, it's an accident, he's shaking so much with the squeezing of a trigger. The men congratulate him. He says nothing. He doesn't say, "It was an accident." Everybody is a coward. Everybody is brave. It's what happens at the moment you do something.

Fixed Bayonets was my first picture for Fox. I met with the heads of all the studios, and [Darryl F.] Zanuck at Fox was the only one who said, "Look, what story do you want to tell?" That's the studio I went with. And I got along great with him. I mean, happiest in my life. He wanted to make a deal for five to seven pictures. I would write, direct, and produce.

Q: But *Park Row*, your next film, was released by United Artists, not Fox. It's a very good newspaper picture, but it doesn't have any kind of genre for people to relate to. It's hard for people to get a hold of it, I think.
A: You say there is something lacking in it to grip you? Zanuck said the same thing when he read it. You said almost word for word what he said before the picture was made. [Zanuck said,] "We made a picture [in 1938] called *In Old Chicago*. It was very successful. [Director] Henry King. Ty Power. Yours we want to call *In Old New York*. Dan Dailey and Mitzi Gaynor. She can play a barmaid, the first barmaid in New York. He can play Steve Brodie. [Gregory] Peck ought to be a composite of all the great newspaper people. And we do it in color. And we do it big. I said, "That's what I don't want. I love *In Old Chicago*. I don't want it to be one of those big things. And in color."

Q: *Pickup on South Street*, maybe your most famous film, was back at Fox. It's got a great opening, hasn't it?
A: Oh, yeah. Everybody thinks that guy is reaching for the crotch. That one was OK'd by Zanuck. I didn't have the yarn. I walked around and said, "I'd like to [figure out these] characters, [who are] very anti-social and on the precipice of crime." The pickpocket? Now, to me a pickpocket is no real criminal, he's an artist. An informer? Yes, she could be a criminal, but that's her job. A girl. Too dumb to be a hooker, too dumb to be a mistress, but she'd do something for a dress. I know girls like that. If you want to use them as a courier, you give them a few dollars and buy them some dresses.

Zanuck said, "That's great. I love these characters. Now who do we root for?" I said, "What do you mean, root for?" He said, "These are horrible characters, but they're so fascinating, they would be good on screen. Who now is their leader?" I give him credit. That's the first time he OK'd anything like that. He OK'd a movie where the people have no taste.

But the interesting thing is the mental and artistic capacity of a petty criminal. I got to know quite a few of them. I trusted them more than anyone in the world. My mother would say, "I'll meet you at two o'clock." She'd be there at 2:30. They are never late, never. When you want information, they're there. They're there ahead of me, waiting. And they don't care what you do. That's their mind, and I love that.

Q: *Pickup on South Street* is about spies, the Cold War. But the people are so apolitical. They get themselves crazily involved with politics, but they don't mean to. It never has any effect on them, does it? No matter what the cops and FBI are onto, these guys are just pursuing their small, narrow human ends.

A: Here is Thelma Ritter being a stool pigeon, always arguing with the cops for more money, and she sells [them] a fellow that's like her son, who she saw grow up. But her job, her profession, is stool pigeon. [The fellow] never gets mad at her. That's her job.

We had two meetings—[Darryl F.] Zanuck, J. Edgar Hoover, and me—at Romanoff's Restaurant. Hoover was against the picture. "We don't have an FBI man there in the presence of an informer. We don't depend on the New York Police Department to depend on informers to get information. Not the Department of Justice!" And he didn't like for [Richard] Widmark to say, "Don't wave the flag at me!" [Hoover] said, "I don't want anyone in this Cold War to say that to anyone, especially cops. The other thing I don't like is [that Widmark] went after [the Communist agent because] the man beat up the girl. He [should have gone] after the man for the United States."

And Zanuck said, "That's [Widmark's] character. [That's Skip.] That's what I like about this guy's story." [Skip] didn't go for all that phony Cold War stuff. He's not interested in politics. You hit the nail on that. They're not even as close as apolitical. They don't give a damn about anything [except] their own little income.

I knew a fellow who lived [like Skip] on the Hudson. No rent. Nobody there. They used to have little shacks like that along the river. They never tore his down. I slept there a lot of times. By the way, [about] the part played by Richard Kiley. He's a Communist agent. But that doesn't mean he's a Communist, a Red. He's a man who, for a dollar, will do what you want on Monday. And Tuesday, if you want him, he becomes your agent.

I wanted to be very, very authentic because I met agents that'll work for anyone. They don't give a damn.

Q: I'd like to talk about *Run of the Arrow*, a remarkable movie. It seems to me to be about how a man, O'Meara, nearly ruins his life by believing too much in a cause. This man, who fought for the South in the Civil War, is so embittered by the lost Rebel cause that he really deserts his country. He goes over to an alien Native culture.

A: He's a symbol of what later became the KKK. A sore loser. This man was brought up in the 1840s and 1850s. Now it's the 1860s. He hates Yankees. [Men like him] were bred so strongly that in World War II, guys were carrying the Confederate flag. He wants to do something á la Robinson Crusoe. Get away from civilization. It's a letdown. Even his own mother [condemns him]: "It's too bad you weren't shot. You shouldn't have come out alive."

Q: You contrast him with the honorable Robert E. Lee.

A: Now, Robert E. Lee . . . a beautiful man, big heart. He was not a bloodthirsty man like Grant was. They [willingly] fought for Lee. Ol' Massah Bob.

Q: O'Meara [Rod Steiger] fires the last shot of the Civil War, wounding a Union officer. He keeps the bullet. Many years later, much has happened, and he uses the bullet a second time, to effect. O'Meara shoots the same guy, who has been captured by his tribe, the Oglalas.

A: He was brought up to hate everyone but Dixie people. But [now] he's an Oglala. The game of Run of the Arrow, they peel [the officer's] balls and they cut his cock off and then they kill him. [O'Meara] with all his hate inside for the Yankees, he can't face this. He's sitting there with all the Oglalas watching a man being peeled to death. He takes that bullet and puts it in [a gun] and kills the officer. That's the only act he performs in this picture that I like, that puts him above hate. I ended it without an end. That's only the beginning. He married an Indian. They're going to have a hell of a tough time in the South.

Q: You cast many real Native Americans in the film.

A: About 120 Sioux, whose ancestors, grandpappy or whatever, fought at Little Big Horn. My description was "No saddles. Ropes. No leather." That's their own ponies. They slept on the ground. They wouldn't sleep in motels. I had to have a little boy in it. I was up in the village there, in the reservation, and I found a kid who was half Comanche. Two brothers representing those 120 Indians, said, "We're Sioux. We don't work with that boy. Devil!"

I got along with them very well, but I made an error. They would roll their long hair up in a bun, and I said, "My mother used to do that." This Indian got very angry. "Don't ever say that . . . a comparison with a woman." I don't know. They're very touchy. I made a speech [to them], and William Dozier, the executive of RKO, was there. I said, "For this final attack, just remember that a man called Custer and his outfit were killed by your people. But remember this too. That's not the last battle." All of this was being translated into their language. "There's the Battle of Wounded Knee, and we killed over three hundred of your civilians. When you charge, you are attacking engineers, and they're protected by infantry, cavalry with guns." I wanted meanness, because I had just insulted them, you see.

Q: What about the casting of Steiger as O'Meara? I think that's interesting.

A: I went for Rod Steiger because of Kazan's picture, *On the Waterfront*. I liked him very much. But the man who owned the Studio [RKO], Tom O'Neill, president of the General Tire Company, wanted Gary Cooper. And he talked to Cooper. I said, "No Cooper! Your sympathy is with him immediately. He's a wonderful man. You love him. He's Gary Cooper. I want a man you're going to hate." When I was in a motel, my cameraman, Joe Biroc, answered the phone. [It was O'Neill.] He said, "I can't sleep. I've been thinking. We'll pay off whoever you wanted. Steiger? This has nothing to do with Steiger. I want Gary Cooper." I said, "Then I'll go somewhere else. I don't want a hero like that. I want a man who looks like I look on a horse. Like a clown. Like nothing, you see." And he gave in.

That man [Steiger] was perfect. He was surly. He looked uncomfortable, he looked like a dirt farmer. He had ANGER. With all due respect to Mr. Cooper, he couldn't give me that anger, that hate.

Q: The "Run of the Arrow," the actual game. How did you come about that?

A: I had a thick book on the etymology of the different languages of the Sioux, and of things they did away from hunting. When they had a "Run of the Arrow"? . . . They didn't like the Cherokee much, they would give them that barefoot run. They had their best marksman shoot an arrow a certain number of yards, and [the captive] would walk to that place. That's the distance [from those chasing after]. If he could lengthen that distance and tire out the people chasing him, he lived. You like that game, don't you?

Q: It's wonderful in the movie. Well, I'd like to talk about another scene that to me is vivid in that same way. That's in your next film, *China Gate*, where the soldiers walk into an ambush, and a man's wounded. They all know he is going to die. And one guy says, "Well, we have to bury you," and the guy says, "Well, yeah." There's a whole dialogue scene: "Well, we can't bury you while you are alive."

A: That's where he says, "I'm sorry I'm taking so long to die." I tried to catch a feeling. [In the War,] we would see a guy like that. We're stuck with him, and we can't move. He gets on our nerves. He's groaning and grunting and gasping, and actually we want him to get it over with. His eyes open, and he sees us looking at him like that. So I thought it would be a nice touch if he apologizes. We saw too many [like him] when we were on the beach. We'd be stuck with him for hours, nowhere to go. Can't go in the water, and [the enemy] is on the cliffs. You're not supposed to help anybody. That's the medics' job. They're the greatest guys in the world, way above the infantry.

Q: What about the love triangle in *China Gate*?

A: I said, "This time, a girl is necessary, she's sleeping with both ends, the French and the Commies." Zanuck: "Do you have a girl in mind?" And I said, "Yes, Angie Dickinson." "Who is she? What has she done?" I said, "I don't know. I used her voice in *Run of the Arrow*." She'd dubbed a voice: I needed a soft voice for this woman. He said, "All right. Okay." He said [about the script], "You make a Commie look pretty good in here. He's educated." I had a line that says, "Ho Chi Minh speaks seven languages. I speak nine. And teachers here don't make any money." Zanuck said: "That's good, because teachers [in America] are always complaining that they are underpaid."

They [Fox] wanted to know who Ho Chi Minh was. I told them. The second assistant pastry chef at the Ritz, in London. And Zanuck said, "You mean a pastry chef is head of a country?" I said, "The second assistant." Zanuck: "I love him because he's Horatio Alger. I'm glad he's head of a country!" What a guy! That's Zanuck, forgetting everything else politically [for] an assistant pastry chef. Then he said, "First thing we'll do is have this big, in CinemaScope, of course. Color." I said, "I want black-and-white." He said, "I'm approving two pictures for you in black-and-white." [*Forty Guns* and *China Gate*] are the only two pictures 20th made [in black-and-white] in CinemaScope.

Zanuck said, "All right, now where will we shoot it?" I said, "I don't want to go on location, Bill Wellman made a great picture, [*The Story of*] *G.I. Joe* at the RKO-Pathè lot, or part of the old Selznick lot, or the inter-marriage of both lots in Culver City. They knocked out a town there. It's supposed to be some town in Italy. With posters of Mao, of Ho, I knew what I could do with that set without touching it. You put up a couple of pictures, huge posters, and you know where you are. [Indo-China.] It was a very unusual [request], because this was 20th Century Fox. They had a great Western lot. They had locations, everything you want. But they didn't have Bill Wellman's set.

Q: It seems to me you've never really wanted to make very expensive movies. You like to work cheaply.
A: I like to work like I made my first three pictures. I rehearse and re-hearse, and shoot once, and I like it. You didn't play around with too much on a newspaper, my God. If a hunch was wrong, your hunch was wrong. That's all. I go by hunches, if a thing smells right. Later on, you're going to talk about *Merrill's Marauders*, that's where I had extras. But I still would handle only a small bunch of men.

Q: In *Forty Guns*, I've rarely seen a cliché overturned so astonishingly as where the bad guy pulls the woman, Barbara Stanwyck, in front of him as a shield, and the other guy just drills them both. I know that the studio said, "All right, she can't be dead. She can only be wounded." Still, it's an amazing moment.
A: Zanuck said she must not die. "We've been making pictures for years, and the hero does not kill the heroine. You've seen *High Noon*. At a very vital moment, Kelly pushes the guy away, and that's when Cooper shoots him." Now how can [Stanwyck] push the guy away? He's holding her with an iron grip. That man [Barry Sullivan] hasn't used a gun in ten years. When he picks up a gun, it's to kill. If that was his mother shield-ing that guy, he'd kill her because he has a gun and doesn't want to use a gun. [Sullivan] said, "Wait a minute, you cannot kill the heroine. I like the picture, but you cannot shoot her. I said, "He's not himself. He's a gun."

Q: But you also supplied a studio ending, as ordered.

A: Zanuck said, "Jesus, now you're making fun of me. That's the old-fashioned type of ending. We've done that for forty years, fifty years. The hero has never killed the heroine." I said, "That's right."

Q: One of the things running through your pictures is a sense of dealing with prejudice, which was, of course, particularly important in the 1950s and '60s. For example, the situation in *The Crimson Kimono*, where a Japanese American detective [James Shigeta], a Nisei, falls in love with an Anglo woman [Victoria Shaw], and his Anglo detective partner [Glenn Corbett] is also in love with her.

A: She goes for the Japanese American, according to my script, because she loves him. I said, "That's it." [Sam Briskin, the Head of Columbia, asked], "Is it possible for the white cop, maybe in one scene, one scene is all I ask for, to be a little bit on the rough side [with her, so she turns to the Japanese cop?]" I said, "No. I know what you are getting at. There will be no reason except that she loves him."

This was not *Broken Blossoms*, a Griffith picture with Richard Barthelmess playing a Chinese fellow. A father is beating the hell out of [his white daughter], and you had to make the Papa a mean son-of-bitch so the girl will turn to the Chinese. I don't like that at all. I never did buy that picture. If her father was a nice man and treated her beautifully, I'd buy that.

I wanted to bring out a central point that there is racism in everybody, here in the Nisei. [He and the white guy] were in Korea together, and the white was saved by the son-of-a-bitch. The Nisei says, "If I were white, you would take this in stride. But because I'm not, it burns you up. It makes you feel little. It makes you feel ashamed." And the white guy says, "Baloney! I don't care who you are!" He says, "You're a racist" to the Nisei. Now that picture, it's not just a chase story or solving a murder. I like something where [a character] should feel a little uncomfortable the way he feels about [another]. That's the beautiful part of a movie. It's entertainment, but at the same time it should be very emotional.

Q: There's a great visual moment near the opening where a frightened stripper runs down the street. It's one of those Fuller moments that is so dislocating.

A: I had a girl, a blonde stripper, 6'2" or 6'3," because I wanted her to stand out. I had a hidden camera in a truck, and she falls in the middle of the street. Traffic is passing. Now the funny part is this: there were American sailors and soldiers walking down Main Street, and an almost naked girl running, and not one of them turned around and looked. In the projection room, one guy said, "What the hell is happening to America today?" So we had to do it again. I didn't want actors [directed] to look at her. I wanted it to be real. By luck, a barber who was shaving came out on the street to look. But the reaction in the projection room was similar. There's something wrong with American men today!

Q: In many of your pictures, and it's maybe a central virtue, you deliberately reverse things, like prejudice being expressed by a Japanese man in *The Crimson Kimono*, the heroine being shot in *Forty Guns*. You are always trying to put a reverse spin on expectations.
A: When I read a book, any book, I read the last line [on a page], and if it's not a finished sentence, I make up what [the author] is going to say. And I turn the page. And if it's nothing that I had in mind, I love it. That's how I want to do a picture. I don't want you to know what you're going to see.

A [bad] movie scene: You tell the girl, "Get me the DA." And [cut], she dials, and says, "District Attorney's Office." Then you cut to the DA's office: "So and so called." And you cut, [third] cut, "This is the DA." I go crazy! I really do. If you have eighty, ninety, one hundred minutes, and it's really tightly packed, each little scene opens up little routes. You take a route, you swing around and hit that route, all hell breaks loose. I like a hit man who thinks he's made it. He just killed somebody. Everything is fine. He walks in and says, "Well, I did it, Ma." And his mother shoots him. That's it. That's the shock. That to me is a hit.

Q: What do you remember of your World War II movie, *Merrill's Marauders*, in the Philippines? The Americans versus the Japanese?
A: I had a gun fight, a fire fight, and we'd shoot each other. A lot of smoke. We'd shoot the enemy. The enemy would shoot each other, and then shoot us. After I shot this fight, Jack Warner called. I was sleeping at Clark Air Base. He said, "I love it. I love it. Except I want to see Japanese getting hit." I said, "Cowboys and Indians." He said, "Exactly. We've been doing that for fifty years." A cavalryman shoots, and an Indian falls. I said, "When you move fast like that in the smoke, you shoot anyone." At the end, he bought it. I'm proud of that shot. When one of the survivors looks down [from above], he can't see who is what and who is killed.

I didn't know anything about the Pacific. I didn't know anything about Merrill. That was from a book by Charlton Ogburn. But it's the only time I showed girls in a war picture. A real war picture, not a trek like *China Gate*. They gave me a chance to show fatigue after a battle. One fellow says, "Girls." He sees some girls in a village. And the other guy says, "Yeah." He does a look. And another character just walks. He walks to a little pond, and just puts his arm down and falls on his face in the water.

Q: Could you talk about the three patients in the mental institution in *Shock Corridor*; the black man who, because of the pressures of racism, now thinks he's in the KKK; a Southern redneck who collaborated with the Communists when captured in Korea; a nuclear scientist guilty about developing the A-Bomb?

A: I thought it would be very interesting to make a picture about three images of the U.S. then, [the early 1960s]. A fellow couldn't go to [a Southern university] because he is black, and a very important statesman stands in the doorway and won't let him in. A [poor white] fellow goes to War, and somebody on the Commie side after he's captured calls him "Mister." And number three, a physicist becomes a vacuum. He has a six-year-old mentality because the thing he was working on, something that could kill masses of people, blows up in his brain. I thought I'd use those as a mirror, a reflection [of America] in a nut house.

The thing of shock art: I couldn't show what I wanted to show. It's in my original script. I couldn't shoot it. [In a mental institution,] they're chained to those benches. Women chained. And men. And they're all naked. They pee there. You can't do that in a Hollywood movie. People would walk out.

There was one reviewer, she was very famous, she didn't like the picture at all. I found out through another reviewer she had someone in her family who was in one of those [hospitals]. She didn't like them being shown. Now, that's not fair. That's personal. If you're a critic, you should like it whether it's a good picture or a bad picture. Did it interest you? Did it enlighten you in any way?

[My wife] Christa picked up the *New York Times*, and there was a story about [James] Meredith, the young man, the black student, who I'd based [my character on in the mental institution]. Meredith said, "I had to quit [the University of Mississippi]. Otherwise, I would have 'gone away.'" Oh, that made me feel funny. This is true.

Q: Can you discuss maybe the single most arresting image you ever made, and that's the opening of *The Naked Kiss*?

A: I open up with a hooker [Constance Towers] fighting her pimp because he held out her money, and she's whacking him with her purse, and her hair falls off, and you find out she was bald. [Maybe] he had cut her hair off to punish her because she wasn't laying enough men. Or [he thought] she was holding back some of the money. Well, let's talk about a technical thing there, and give him his due. Stanley Cortez, the cameraman. He's wonderful, wonderful. He did *Shock Corridor* for me. I said to Stanley, "I know it's easy for you. Hand-held camera. But [instead] I'd like for the man to have the camera strapped to him when she beats him. And I'd like for her to have the camera strapped on her breast, when you see the purse going." And we did that. The biggest worry we had was the cameras were so heavy, and these are actors, you see.

Show it! Don't talk about it! I didn't want to say, "She's an honest whore." [Instead,] she beats the hell out of [her pimp], he's semi-conscious, she takes out his roll, takes what's due to her, and throws the rest of the money in his face. That shows her character. That's a good way to open a picture.

Q: Later in the film, the prostitute, Kelly, is thrown in jail for murder, with everyone in a small town against her. But they suddenly embrace her when it's learned that the man she killed was a child molester.

A: Now they want her to stay, she wants to go back to the clean, fresh breath of air of whoring. And to a big city. In little towns we didn't do any business at all, because I have her speaking right into the camera. "You're all hypocrites." I had a stronger speech than that, but [the Studio] said, "Why don't we go a little easy on this? You're speaking about a chairman of the board of aldermen, and the aldermen, and mayors. Kind of leave that out, will you?"

Q: I've heard that John Wayne wanted to play The Sergeant in *The Big Red One* (1980), but you were reluctant to use him.

A: I said, "First I have to go look for locations. I don't know. I haven't got a hook." And [Jack] Warner said, "What is a hook?" I said, "A hook is what the story is. S-T-O-R-Y. It's not just a lot of fighting." Then I kept stalling. Meanwhile, Oscar Dystel came out from New York. He's an editor at Bantam. He said, "If you're going to do *The Big Red One*, do it as a book. You can do it as a movie later." Now it had reached the point where I was embarrassed. Every time I saw Wayne he said, "Where is the script?

The hell with the book." Dystel said, "The hell with the picture." And then I got the hook. And the hook, of course, is survivors. Each survivor could represent fifteen thousand men.

Now Wayne, who I liked, was wrong for The Sergeant. I wanted a tired man from World War I. A man sapped out of everything, but, above all, who represents death. Gaunt. Bony. And then I met Lee Marvin at the Witness Tobacco Shop. I said, "I am working on a script. You're the guy for it." "Ah, you tell that it to every son-of-a-bitch you meet in the cigar store," he said. And when it came time to cast, the one they wanted was Steve McQueen. He was very hot. I said, "Wrong. Wrong age. He'd have been eleven in World War II." Lee Marvin was in New Mexico. He called me and said, "This is your Sergeant," and hung up. I was very happy because he was cast right. He was wise, he was experienced, he was cold.

Q: Even in *The Big Red One*, you work in an insane asylum.
A: They're going to knock off a German observation post in the attic of an insane asylum in Belgium, and the young fellow, Mark Hamill, says to Marvin, "Why the hell do we have to go in there? Why don't we blow up the goddamned thing?" Marvin says, "Naw, there are insane people in there." And the kid says, "You mean it's wrong for us to kill insane people?" "That's right. It's wrong." "But it's okay to kill sane people?" "Yes." Now that's war!

Q: We need to talk about *White Dog* (1982), which seems to me one of your most important movies.
A: Yeah, it wasn't shown in theatres by Paramount. I feel very strong about that story. It's strictly an anti-racist story. It's an exposé of Mama and Papa and Grandpapa. And my old flag. I wave that flag all the time. It's the parents who are responsible [for teaching racism]. It's how a kid is reared, like the dog was raised to hate and attack [anyone] black.

It may be ten generations from now, fifty generations, where people will say, "You mean to say that someone did so-and-so to someone because of his color?" That's like us saying, "Do you mean in the Coliseum midgets would come out with naked women and they'd fight each other?" We think it's crude or moronic, or animalistic or cannibalistic.

Q: *White Dog* comes from a story by the French novelist, Romain Gary, doesn't it?
A: He wrote an autobiography that was published in its entirety in *Life* magazine, when [publisher] Henry Luce was alive, with a cover of *White*

Dog. The whole story. It's about himself and his wife [actress Jean Seberg] and the Black Panthers, this and that. I threw all that out. That's for a gossip column. I'm not worried about your personal life at all. Couldn't interest me. You want to sleep with a horse, you sleep with a horse. It doesn't bother me. I don't like meddling in anyone's personal likes or dislikes. So I made it a simple story of how a dog is trained, and how a black man tries to retrain that dog.

Q: We are in Paris. You are the most American of Americans. How come you are living here?
A: Well, I came here for the opening of *White Dog*. Here it's called a masterpiece. The *London Times*: "Magnificent." Not [so in] America. For personal reasons, we remained here. My little kid got sick, so we stayed. I could live anywhere. I don't give a damn. My little kid misses California. We're [also] renting a house in Hollywood.

Q: Here in France, your films have been reevaluated and highly praised. You are probably familiar with what François Truffaut wrote about them. I think what he's saying is, your pictures are not primitive and not crude, but they are rude. He's saying, you cut through a lot of bullshit. You get to very, very basic emotions.
A: Well, I never had that translated for me. All I knew is that it was complimentary.

Q: But you can feel that you are more appreciated in France than the USA?
A: Well, they did that even before I got here. It's good for my ego, which is normal. But the thing is, I don't care where I am. I even made a film in Mexico, and we lived there for a year. I went to—where the hell is it?—Portugal, and made one there. And now I just finished one here.

Q: To you, what is a director?
A: You give him a sandwich, and it's rounded into a hell of a dinner. That to me is a director. A director is a creator who chooses to create with a camera, who shouldn't be hog-tied by [adapting] a novel. Now, they say, of course, you can't photograph a novel. You can't photograph thoughts. You can. A camera can do anything you want. Now I've known directors who've taken ordinary scripts and made them brilliant, like Welles doing it in *Touch of Evil*. But a director [doesn't necessarily have] to change anything. It's like an extremely good editor. He does not alter your work.

I don't think it's necessary to [make changes] if you have a great scene from Dostoyevsky, or Dickens's [*David*] *Copperfield*, or Balzac gone crazy. Anything Edgar Poe wrote is visual. Anything O'Henry wrote is visual.

A director is someone who puts things on screen visually. There might be fifteen or twenty pages of dialogue. Visually, it's five seconds on the screen. A director conceives what is the highlight of a story. *War and Peace* doesn't have to take eight or ten hours. What is a highlight Tolstoy wanted to bring out? And how can we show it where we don't lose the progress of characters? A director must be infested with emotion. He should pinpoint an emotion and milk it, and not bore anyone with it.

I saw [Laurence] Olivier, a few of his Shakespeare [productions]. I love him! I thought they were great. He gave them flesh and blood. *Storm over Asia* [1928], a Russian picture. [V. I.] Pudovkin was the director. A group of men, and they are going to attack the cavalry. You get a few good stuntmen and you've got the damned horses, and you do it. But Pudovkin . . . he had the wind blowing high grass toward you. The wind is coming in. Sssshh! Then the strength and power of those hoofs made the grass go that way! Aaagh! That's storytelling. And it's visual!

A director has always been compared to an orchestra conductor, and I think that's nonsense. [He is] following something note for note for note. A director of a film will add notes. A director can do that with the camera. Visual emotion. A director takes a song and he makes a symphony out of it. Does that make sense to you?

Q: That's great. Thanks. That's it!

Seven Questions for Foreign Filmmakers Shooting in France

Hubert Niogret, Michel Ciment, Philippe Rouyer, Jean A. Gili/1988

From *Positif* 325 (March 1988): 43, 50–51. Reprinted by permission.

Q: Why did you decide to shoot a film, *Les Voleurs de la Nuit/Thieves After Dark*, outside of your country? Why did you choose France?
A: I have made movies in Japan, in the Philippines, in Israel, in Ireland. Why not in Paris?

Q: Was one of the reasons the image of French cinema?
A: I came to Paris at the request of Paramount to prepare for the premiere of *White Dog*.

Q: What has been your experience with producing in France? In what way has this changed your work methods?
A: Shooting here has not changed my methods of working.

Q: What have been the positive and/or negative aspects of the production mechanisms in French cinema that you have been able to take advantage of? In what ways has this been different from your previous experiences making *Les Voleurs de la Nuit* in France?
A: The positive points: Philippe Rousselot on camera, Dominique André as art director, Catherine Kelber as editor, as well as the producers, the assistant director, Rosalie Varda's costumes, François Andrejak's make-up, Margot Capelier in charge of casting, and every man and woman on the crew. The negative points: the translation from English to French by Anne and George Dutter for the final presentation was a bit rushed.

Q: What has been your experience with French technical crews, and in what way does this differ from your other experiences?
A: They are top-notch professionals. Language was not an obstacle. For example: the art director, Dominique André, didn't speak English. I don't speak French. But he sensed what I wanted and immediately did what was necessary. For me, this was a significant experience, proving that film is international, that an object has no homeland, and that people who have cinema coursing through their veins make shooting a real pleasure.

Q: What were your feelings about the media and press in France when your French film, *Les Voleurs de la Nuit*, debuted here? Was this experience different than with previous releases?
A: With a few exceptions, the French press hated the film. At the [1984] festival in Berlin, it was a disaster. Confronting these critics was a memorable time for me. A young man declared that the film wasn't "realistic," that it was just a cliché. His platitudes were funny to me: the clichés were he and his speech. He considered himself to be an artist, an intellectual, a messenger of the avant-garde. But showing a lack of intelligence, of imagination, of experience, he didn't know that the word "realistic" has no place in a show business. Of course, there's simulated realism through storytelling tricks and stage effects. Actual "realism"?—that would be a war film where a gunman hides behind the screen and blows off a spectator's ear. That wouldn't boost ticket sales, but the audience wouldn't have any doubts as to the role of "realism" in projecting the film. Cinematographic fiction can approach "realism," because fiction is more real than the truth. Sometimes fiction is more realistic than "realism." But the word "realism," in my opinion, is too heavy for the world of show business.

The fact that the shooting of the film occurred in France didn't really change anything. The changes had to do with [me making a drama about] unemployment, a tragedy felt all over the world. In this movie, the men and women who interview the boy [Bobby De Cicco] and girl [Vèronique Jannot] who are looking for work are pretentious little dictators. Their authoritarian styles lay out the [grim] future for these young people.

I had another reason for making this film: to show that young people everywhere should trust the police, not try to run away from them, especially when the youth are innocent. Fleeing leads to a tragic outcome. Not all cops are pigs. But a single rotten apple in the basket is enough to ruin the reputation of every cop. One jerk police who abuses his authority and breaks down a young person looking for work, that's a rotten apple in comparison to the other authority figures who are trying to help someone find a job, and to be friendly, helpful, and encouraging.

I was obviously disappointed that the French press didn't like my first film made in France. But [people's disapproval] has already happened to me. For example: racists hated *White Dog* because I underlined that what makes a racist is a father or mother who teaches hate to his children. I questioned members of the Ku Klux Klan and [that was a key factor] of their hostility: they had been nurtured with hate and animosity toward a certain color or religion. The teaching of hate is a fact. Thanks to a movie, I [had an opportunity] to touch upon the reality of this cancer, a cancer that can be defeated if future generations stop teaching hate to children.

Another example of taste and distaste: in *The Steel Helmet* I portrayed an American soldier who aims at and kills a Chinese Communist prisoner of war. Uncle Sam didn't appreciate that, but it doesn't change the fact that that it was based on reality. It was in the middle of the Cold War, and that cold was heating up, and then burning, because bullets were replacing words. I used this image of a man who kills a prisoner of war to break down all the romantic and glorified aspects of combat, no matter what the cause or country that is being defended. They say that war has rules, but since war is organized insanity, I don't see any rules in that fog of madness. Lieutenant Calley, for example, massacred a crowd of civilians [in Vietnam]. They said he was sick. But sickness is no excuse. Neither is insanity.

Reactionaries called me a "Communist" and "comrade" for that scene in *The Steel Helmet*, and it was applauded by the Communist newspapers, the *Daily Worker* and *The People's World*. But they ripped me to shreds for other parts of the film which showed them in a less than favorable light, and they said that Douglas MacArthur had backed me! Certain critics think that when I write a film, I am expressing my own political opinions. This is absurd. And George Sadoul, a left-winger, a masterful critic, apparently, called me a reactionary. Absurd! I don't know what he did during the War, but I fought against the fascists for three years, and I was wounded. I've always shown both sides of an issue because, for me, *that's* "realism."

One more example: *Pickup on South Street.* The Cold War was in full force and J. Edgar Hoover objected to the scene where an American fighter pilot refuses to cooperate with Uncle Sam, who's looking for an important microfilm which was about to be sold to Russia for $25,000. Hoover objected to what the pilot says to the FBI, "It'll do no good to wave your flag in my face!" Hoover just wanted propaganda speeches. Mr. Hoover disapproved of the fact that the pilot turns over the microfilm not for his country, but to save the woman he loves.

I am a Jeffersonian Democrat, I've always voted Democrat, I don't like mundane liberals from any country, or socialite reactionaries from any country. To me, combating the Ku Klux Klan is more than a fight for liberalism; it's an international battle against racism.

Q: What do you think of French cinematographic creation today?
A: Today's French cinematographic artists are magnificent!

Interview with Samuel Fuller: "I Was at the Premiere of *Dracula*"

François Guerif/1988

From *La Revue du Cinéma* 437 (April 1988): 79–80. Reprinted by permission of François Guerif.

Q: How did you end up with a role in *Return to Salem's Lot*?
A: It all started with a conversation between director Larry Cohen and me about Nazi hunters, who became vampire hunters in the film. He wrote the part for me.

Q: What interested you about the script?
A: I liked the idea of a film about children and vampires. I don't really know if the idea comes through clearly, but it's the first film about children's sexuality. The vampires are adults who never grew up. It's original.

Q: Do you like the horror genre?
A: I like it a whole lot. Along with film noir, it's the genre that ages the best. I remember going to the [1930] premiere of *Dracula* with my mother. Universal Pictures had made sure that there were nurses in the lobby, and an ambulance behind the theatre in case anyone felt ill.

Q: Were you scared?
A: We were absolutely terrified. You can't imagine the effect Bela Lugosi had on us!

Q: Why haven't you made any horror films yourself?
A: The only thing that I don't like about the genre is that it's the same story, over and over and over. To me, a horror story has to be original, like *The Fly*. But after the third or fourth *Dracula* or *Frankenstein*, the genre

starts to go downhill. If you put Dracula and Frankenstein in the same movie, neither one of them benefits from the situation. I became friends with Lon Chaney, Jr. He was raising rabbits on his ranch. He was never really involved with the genre, unlike his father.

Q: But would you make a horror film today?
A: I don't know. I haven't been following the genre's evolution in the past few years. If I agreed to make Larry Cohen's movie, it's also because I went back to New England, a place I hadn't set foot in years.

Q: What do you think are the masterpieces of the genre?
A: James Whale's *Frankenstein*, Tod Browning's *Dracula*. With these two films, Universal invented everything.

Additional Bibliography

Amiel, Olivier. *Samuel Fuller*. Paris: Henri Veyrier, 1985.

Beylie, Claude, and J. Lourcelles. "Sam Fuller Returns." *Écran* (Paris) no. 32 (January 1975), 52–62.

Bochicchio, Gisella, and B. Roberti. "Conversazione con Samuel Fuller." *Siena* 40 (September–October 1989), 542–44.

Dombrowski, Lisa. *The Films of Samuel Fuller: If You Die, I'll Kill You!* Middletown, Conn.: Wesleyan University Press, 2008.

Eyquem, Olivier, and Michael Henry. "D'une guerre l'autre: entretien avec Samuel Fuller." *Positif* (Paris) 244/245 (July 1981), 62–70.

Farber, Manny. *Negative Space*. New York: Praeger Publishers, 1971.

Fuller, Samuel, with Christa Lang Fuller and Jerome Henry Rudes. *A Third Face: My Tale of Writing, Fighting, and Filmmaking*. New York: Alfred A. Knopf, 2002.

Garnham, Nicholas. *Samuel Fuller*. New York: The Viking Press, 1971.

Guerif, François. *Sans Espoir de Retour*. Paris: Henri Veyrier, 1989.

Hardy, Phil. *Samuel Fuller*. New York: Praeger Publishers, 1970.

Hillier, Jim, ed. *Cahiers du Cinéma, The 1950s: Neo-Realism, Hollywood, New Wave*. Cambridge, Mass.: Harvard University Press, 1985.

Hoberman, J. "Sam Fuller: Gate Crasher at the Auteur Limits." *The Village Voice*, July 2, 1980, 39.

Hunter, Allan. "An Interview with Sam Fuller." *Films and Filming* 350 (November 1983), 9–10.

Jacobson, Mark. "This Gun for Hire." *The Village Voice*, August 30, 1976, 61, 63, 65.

Krohn, Bill, and Barbara Frank. "Entretien avec Samuel Fuller." *Cahiers du Cinéma* 311 (May 1980), 15–23.

Milne, Tom, ed. *Godard on Godard*. New York: The Viking Press, 1972.

Monder, Eric. "A Fuller View: An Interview with Sam Fuller." *Filmfax* 49 (March/April 1995), 73–76.

Narboni, Jean, and Noel Simsolo. *Il Etait Une Fois . . . Sam Fuller*. Paris: C.D.C., 1986.

Porfirio, Robert, Alain Silver, and James Ursini. "Interviews with Samuel Fuller," *Film Noir Reader 3*. New York: Limelight Editions, 2002.

Sarris, Andrew. *The American Cinema*. New York: E. P. Dutton & Co., 1968.

Server, Lee. *Samuel Fuller: Film Is a Battleground*. Jefferson, N.C.: McFarland & Company, Inc., 1994.

S.L.P. "Fuller Mis au Défi par L'avocat du Diable." *Cahiers du Cinéma* 334–335 (April 1982), 76–83.

Thompson, Richard. "3 X Sam: The Flavor of Ketchup." *Film Comment*, January–February, 1977, 24–31.

Truffaut, François. *The Films in My Life*. New York: Simon & Schuster, 1978.

Will, David, and Peter Wollen, eds. *Samuel Fuller*. Edinburgh: Edinburgh Film Festival, 1969.

Index

Printed in the United States
by Baker & Taylor Publisher Services